"What Brian Croft and Ronnie
ministers here is astounding—a de
reaches into the humanity of pastoral ministry while remaining
rooted in the supernaturalizing ministry of the gospel. Slow down,
read it prayerfully, and have your heart strengthened by grace."

Jared C. Wilson
Assistant Professor, Pastoral Ministry, and Author-in-Residence,
Midwestern Baptist Theological Seminary; Pastor for Preaching and
Director, Pastoral Training Center, Liberty Baptist Church;
Author, *Gospel-Driven Ministry*

"*The Unhurried Pastor* provides a practical and biblical prescription
for a healthy and productive pastoral ministry in the face of a
discouraging diagnosis and pathetic prognosis of pastoral
ministry. With their weathered honesty, authors Brian Croft and
Ronnie Martin urge pastors to be about their Father's business
in an unhurried manner. Their work offers fresh, new ways
for traditional and nontraditional pastors to reclaim spiritual
disciplines that prioritize *being* over *doing* while encouraging
sustainable pastoral journeys."

Dr. Robert Smith, Jr.
Charles T. Carter Baptist Chair of Divinity, Beeson Divinity School,
Samford University

"This book is much more than a compendium of tips to slow down
your life and ministry. It is an invitation to minister not just at
the pace of Jesus but also in the presence of Jesus. Written from
a trial-and-error perspective, Ronnie and Brian honestly examine
how the practices of contemplation, prayer, and silence can work
against our ingrained habits of speed and productivity in order
to take us deeper into the wisdom of God. More importantly,
they repeatedly draw out insight from Scripture to recalibrate our
hearts to hum with grace. I hope you'll read this book and pray as
insights land on you in each chapter, so you can be formed on the
spot by God's beautifying word."

Jonathan K. Dodson
Theologian-in-Residence, Citizens Church;
Author, *The Unwavering Pastor*

"*The Unhurried Pastor* is a helpful and needed foundational guide for assisting pastors in structuring their life and work as a pastor. Brian Croft and Ronnie Martin's wisdom offers a practical road map for forming a rule of life for pastors that will prevent pastoral burnout while fostering a truly Christ-centered human approach to pastoral ministry that has staying power and presence. This book is an essential read for young pastors and a needed refresher for pastors with years of ministry."

Richard Plass
Founder, CrossPoint Ministry

Brian Croft and Ronnie Martin

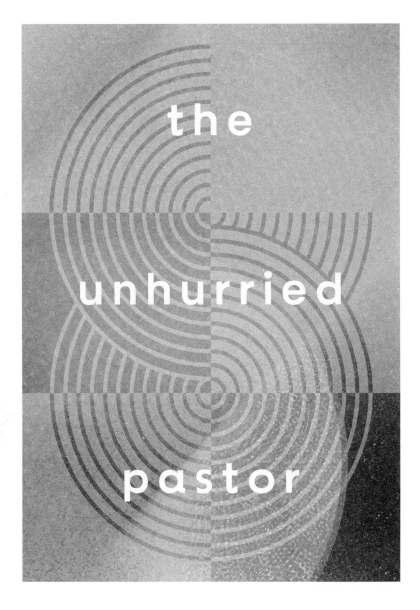

the

unhurried

pastor

thegoodbook
COMPANY

To the late Eugene Peterson,
upon whose unhurried shoulders we now stand.

Contents

Introduction

BY BRIAN CROFT

Bob stepped into my office. He was in his mid-forties with about 15 years of hard pastoral ministry under his belt. He had a look of despair in his eyes as he shared why he had come: "I'm holding on by a thread. I don't think I can do this much longer. I'm not sleeping much. I work all the time, but now struggle to even hold thoughts in my head to write a sermon. I have no joy in my work, which I once loved. Some days, I can barely get out of bed."

That same week Sam, another pastor in his forties, called me on the phone to talk: "I just got back from the emergency room. My wife took me because I thought I was having a heart attack. They ran tests and confirmed my heart was fine but told me that I had experienced a panic attack. Until recently I had never had a panic attack in my life, and yet now it happens every time I drive to the church. I haven't preached in the pulpit since. I don't know what is happening or what to do." Unfortunately, these are all too common scenarios, which Ronnie and I (Brian) both face in our ministry to pastors.

It is no secret that we are in the middle of an time of unprecedented pastoral burnout. Here are just a few of the startling statistics:

- 42% of pastors considered quitting in the last year.[1]
- 50% of pastors do not make it to five years in the ministry.[2]
- 80% of pastors do not last ten years in the ministry.[3]

These numbers are taken from the US but similar statistics show that this is not just an American problem. Such numbers reveal many things, but here are two primary observations about why so many pastors have such seemingly short tenures. First, being a pastor is just hard. There are the demands of 24/7 availability. The pressures of the workload. The mental toll of preparing several sermons or teachings every week. The emotional anguish that accompanies bearing the burdens of suffering people, while also carrying your own personal burdens. The financial compensation is commonly not adequate. Added to all this, pastors are trying to love and care for sinners—many are redeemed sinners, but they are still sinners. The fights, criticisms, complaints, conflicts, and petty disagreements that pastors moderate is enough to cause a relatively healthy person to lose their minds. The work of pastoral ministry is uniquely hard, and it always has been.

But second, the way modern pastors engage with their ministry is unsustainable in the long-term. These numbers reveal an undeniable flaw in the manner in which the 21st-century pastor does the work of ministry. The rest of this book will unpack this dynamic, but here it is in brief: in our work with many depressed, burned-out pastors, we see that the common link between them is an inability to see their limitations and embrace them. Whether it's because of the expectations placed upon us by our church's culture or our own internal drive (or a combination of the two), too many of us operate as if we are superhuman. The problem is that we are not superhuman.

Now, thankfully, this reality has begun to get the attention of the broader evangelical movement and the churches these pastors serve. There now exists a growing number of ministries seeking to address the care of pastors and their families. In fact, both of us serve with ministries trying to accomplish this very thing.[4] We see a growing number of churches learning to better care for their pastors, creating capacity for breaks and sabbaticals, and providing resources for mentoring and counseling. There are encouraging signs that Bible colleges, seminaries, and other pastoral-training institutes, are also waking up to the need to care for pastors, and for that, we are thankful.

However, despite the progress and attention now being given to the care of pastors in the ministry, as well as of those aspiring to it, this still does not solve the greater problem. The greater problem is a long-held acceptance of how pastors are expected to do their ministry in the modern era.

And it is not sustainable.

The Prophetic Voice of Eugene Peterson

Eugene Peterson was the pastor of Christ Our King Presbyterian Church in Bel Air, Maryland for almost three decades and the author of many books. You may recognize his name as the author of *The Message* Bible paraphrase. Or you might only know Peterson from a few controversies that popped up on social media in the final years of his life.[5]

But what you are less likely to know is that Eugene Peterson was one of the first to push against the busy, noisy, frantic, and unsustainable ministry practice that pastors in his generation were expected to embrace. Without a doubt, this ministry approach still exists on steroids today.

In the late 1980s, Peterson wrote a book entitled *The Contemplative Pastor*, which included a chapter he called "The Unbusy Pastor". Some years before this, Peterson was a self-confessed "busy pastor," which eventually brought him to the brink of burning out and quitting. But he didn't quit. Instead, he made some significant changes in his life and schedule and, most importantly, to his understanding of the work of a pastor and what he needed to do to be truly faithful in it:

> It was a favorite theme of C. S. Lewis that only lazy people work hard. By lazily abdicating the essential work of deciding and directing, establishing values and setting goals, other people do it for us; then we find ourselves frantically, at the last minute, trying to satisfy a half dozen different demands on our time, none of which is essential to our vocation, to stave off the disaster of disappointing someone. But if I vainly crowd my day with conspicuous activity or let others fill my day with imperious demands, I don't have time to do my proper work, the work to which I have been called. How can I lead people into the quiet place beside the still waters if I am in perpetual motion? How can I persuade a person to live by faith and not by works if I have to juggle my schedule constantly to make everything fit into place?[6]

Peterson's resolution to resist the commonly accepted uber-busy life of a pastor was prophetic for two main reasons. First, he saw the unsustainability of this even in his day and had the courage and foresight to push against it. He saw with spiritual eyes where it would lead. This one chapter of *The Unbusy Pastor*, which was also published as a *Christianity Today* article, remains one of the clearest flags of warning to a pastor of his statistically probable demise.

Second, what makes Peterson's observations all the more remarkable is that they predate the internet. And yet, if this redefining of the pastoral work was ever needed, it is now! In the last few decades, the internet and social media have caused an already busy, hurried, and unsustainable approach to pastoral ministry to become *even busier*, more hurried, and more unsustainable. Peterson could not have imagined how fast the world would change with this one tool, and how it would create a perfect technological storm heightening the pressure, the demands, the conflict, the expectations, and the isolation for pastors in the ministry.

We believe we find ourselves in this current crisis because we have ignored for far too long what Eugene Peterson saw long ago. Now, more than ever, the prophetic voice of Eugene Peterson in this regard needs to be heard. In light of his recent death, we want to take up his call and continue to sound the note that he did in his generation—*that is, a redefining of how the work of a pastor is done so that it will lead to joy and longevity for the pastor.*

The Purpose of This Book

This is what we hope to accomplish with this book. *The Unhurried Pastor* is not a call to redefine the work of a pastor. The biblical understanding of the call of a pastor is, if anything, growing clearer and clearer with this younger generation of pastors: that is, "to shepherd the flock of God that is among you" (1 Peter 5:2). *The Unhurried Pastor* is, however, a call—a plea, really—to redefine how this work is accomplished. This will be an uphill battle for sure. It is a push against the accepted busy and frantic practice of pastors today, as well as a push against our broader Western mindset, which assumes that to be productive we must always be busy, moving, and hurried.

Our aim is to convince you that the secret to true, spiritual fruitfulness is in fact the opposite. Genuine pastoral productivity—of a kind that brings joy and longevity—is unlocked through the practices reflected in some of the titles of chapters that follow: humanity, humility, self-awareness, prayer, contemplation, silence, rest, friendship. We will challenge you about these things. We will address many of the practicalities. But in this book you will not find a blueprint to be more productive by being busier. The secret to true productivity in the work of the kingdom, as we walk with Christ and shepherd his people, lies in *being* more than *doing*. If we convince you to reconsider your own approach to the work of the ministry, we will be pleased.

So where do we start? Let's have Eugene Peterson set the tone for what you should expect as you begin this book. You might be wondering, "If I shouldn't do things the way I have always done them, or the way I have been trained to do them, then what *should* I do?" Peterson addresses that question as follows:

> If I'm not busy making my mark in the world or doing
> what everyone expects me to do, what do I do? What
> is my proper work? What does it mean to be a pastor?
> If no one asked me to do anything, what would I do?
> Three things. I can be a pastor who prays. I can be a
> pastor who preaches. I can be a pastor who listens ... I
> mark out the times for prayer, for reading, for leisure,
> for the silence and solitude out of which creative work—
> prayer, preaching, and listening—can issue.[7]

Pastors, if these words resonate with your weary soul—if you're longing for a more joyful and sustainable rhythm of ministry—keep reading. And if these words make your hurried, frantic soul feel slightly nervous—you should keep reading too. Imagine a different pace when you arrive at your church premises or sit at your desk on Monday morning. Imagine being able to pray, or study, or be present with a church member without that frantic awareness of what is coming next. If this appeals to you—keep reading. Trust that Jesus will meet you where you are and minister his grace to you as you wrestle with this alongside us. Be assured, we are learning with you.

A Final Word of Irony

Ronnie and I are painfully aware of two specific ironies that almost sabotaged the writing and completion of this book. First, we were both "too busy" to work on this to get it done. (We know. Don't stare.) Second, we wrestled on many occasions with the belief that we are not equipped or qualified to write such a book. We are not experts in doing ministry in a present, still, unhurried, thoughtful manner. Not many are. But in our combined 45 years of pastoral ministry, we have run long and hard, flamed out, got back up, made changes, and tasted the benefits. We hope you too might taste the benefits as you read, and we hope to grow in our own lives as we write. So, let's step out on this journey together with the hope that joy and longevity await us all.

Part 1

Preparation

By Ronnie Martin

CHAPTER ONE

Humanity

"I am a human being."

Sigh.

There, I said it.

Now you go ahead and say it out loud, if you can.

I am a human being.

The funny thing is that I'm not sure I know anybody who needs to embrace those five words more than you right now. And, to be clear, by "you" I actually mean *me.*

When I write about "pastors" in this book, I want you to know that I'm talking about myself. I may be the writer of these words, but I need them as much as, if not more than, you. So, in order to embrace my own humanity as I begin writing a chapter on "humanity," you all should know that I believe I'm the first person who needs to do just that.

Will you pause with me for one second though? Did you notice how I just said "person," not "pastor"? This might be one of the most important distinctions I will make throughout this whole chapter and that you will make in your ministry. The reality is that most of us try to shepherd like superheroes—but the problem is that there's nothing superhuman about us.

Before I assume the title of pastor, shepherd, elder, preacher, teacher, author, speaker, or counselor, I am a *person* who is fearfully and wonderfully made in the image of God. To take another step back, I am a descendant of Adam, whom God formed from the dust of the earth. Thankfully, I'm made up of redeemed dust and earth now—redeemed not so that I might become the greatest *pastor* that ever walked the earth but so that I can return to being the kind of *person* God originally created to walk the earth.

Trouble is, you might know that that makes sense theologically, but it's another thing entirely for it to translate practically.

The Humanity We've Been Dealt

Brian referenced this in our introduction, but there was a point before we began writing this book when I told him that I wasn't sure we should. When you look at the pace of our lives, the words "hurried pastor," not "unhurried pastor," should be what's printed on the coffee mugs we hurriedly drink from. He graciously reminded me that, in fact, we are the perfect people (ok, not *perfect*, but you know what I mean) to be writing on this topic because of how deeply we struggle to embody the very essence of unhurriedness ourselves.

I posted this thought on social media after our exchange:

I'm currently coauthoring a book on the unsustainable pace of pastors—as I struggle with my own unsustainable pace.

On one hand I think, "I should not be writing this."

On the other hand I think, "Who better to write this?"

Writers should be those who wrestle like no other.

The truth is that I wrestle like crazy with this whole "humanity" thing. Embracing my humanity feels boring, average, mundane, uninspiring, and full of opportunities to not live up to the potential that I imagine for myself as a 21st-century pastor. I don't want to see myself for who I truly am: someone with emotional issues, family-of-origin issues, physical limitations, spiritual blind spots, and a whole bunch else. It's easier to *just keep moving.*

If that doesn't create enough complexities, here's another thing: I fear my congregation doesn't really want to see me as I truly am either. They want to see a *pastor*, not a *person*.

Now, I hear where your thoughts are going right now: "Ronnie, congregations nowadays want a pastor who is not afraid to be a vulnerable and transparent person. Why can't he be both?"

Admittedly, there's some truth to that. We want to see our pastors preaching from a place of weathered honesty, like David the psalmist, laying themselves low before the Lord and their people, and staying as far away from that spiritual pedestal as possible. I'm all in on that, by the way.

But, I wonder…

I wonder how easy it is to curate an image of ourselves as a "vulnerable and transparent" pastor in such a way that our membership status as a superhero in the Marvel Evangelical Universe remains intact to our congregation? In other words, it's possible to present oneself as a vulnerable and transparent *pastor*, rather than a vulnerable and transparent *person*.

And—man, oh man—is there a difference.

A good sign that you are not merely curating an image of the "vulnerable and transparent pastor" is how vulnerable and transparent you are before the Lord. Are you becoming more psalmist-like in the way you lay yourself, humble and low, before the Lord, or do you find yourself unconsciously obscuring your humanity before him?

The truth is that your people have likely been taught to deal with you as a pastor instead of as a human being who happens to have been called to pastor them.

Here's a question to ponder: What do you think would happen if you presented yourself to your congregation as a *person* before doing that as their *pastor*? What if you took the risk of learning how to share more of yourself with your congregation—not in a way that makes every sermon about you but in a way that allows them to feel a greater kinship with how you experience and respond to God's word? How would people react if you offered them your true self: an ultra-fragile, incredibly limited, profoundly average, and disappointingly human human being? What do you think would happen?

The problem is that we are scared to death of finding out. Fear makes it "easier" for us to show up as a *pastor* instead of a *person*—until, that is, it becomes the hardest thing in the world to do and we become exhausted by the demands of denying the very thing we were created to be: a human being.

Some of the consequences that come with this way of living and being will be paranoia ("I wonder what everyone's really thinking about me?"), bitterness ("I will never meet people's expectations"), and disillusionment ("No matter what I do, things will never change"). When these negative internal emotions become the fuel we run on, we can't go on for long.

So what's the way forward? To answer that question, we need to look back.

Origin Story

There's a reason why we love origin stories. And why movie studios like them too. I remember, at the end of the 90s, when it was announced that George Lucas was going to be making three new prequels to his iconic Star Wars trilogy. For kids of the 70s and 80s (including me), we could hardly believe this was really happening. Finally, we were going to get the untold story of how Darth Vader became, well, Darth Vader. And that's what we love about origin stories—learning what made a person the person they've become.

The story of Adam and Eve in Genesis 2 and 3 is the origin of all origin stories. It helps us understand the roots of why we aspire to be more-than-human pastors—so that we can avoid becoming less-than-human persons. When I say "less-than-human," I'm referring to our tendency to live *other than* in the way that God designed us to—a tendency which denies and diminishes our humanity. As we'll see, God intentionally created us with limitations as a way for his divine glory and our human flourishing to be better experienced and enjoyed.

Genesis 2 shows us a time when humans were untainted by sin and therefore able to live out their God-given humanity in the most perfect way imaginable. There are some subtle things for us to notice as Adam enters the workplace for the first time:

> *The LORD God took the man and put him in the garden of Eden to work it and keep it. And the LORD God commanded the man, saying, "You may surely eat of every tree of the garden, but of the tree of the knowledge of good and evil you shall not eat, for in the day that you eat of it you shall surely die."*

> *Then the LORD God said, "It is not good that the man should be alone; I will make him a helper fit for him." Now out of the ground the LORD God had formed every beast of the field and every bird of the heavens and brought them to the man to see what he would call them. And whatever the man called every living creature, that was its name. The man gave names to all livestock and to the birds of the heavens and to every beast of the field.*

> *(Genesis 2:15-20)*

It's like you can almost hear God saying, *Adam, you have one job. Be the person I made you to be in this garden paradise called Eden.* Pay close attention to the phrasing: God "took" Adam and "put" him in the garden. It was *God's* job to place Adam, and it was Adam's job to keep the garden God had placed him in. The differentiation between those two roles is critical. Part of Adam's responsibility was also to obey the word God had commanded. His humanity depended on it, just as ours does.

As pastors, we need to remember that, in a similar way, God took us and placed us to keep the church, which he prevents the gates of hell from prevailing upon. Acts 20:28 tells us to "care for the church of God, which he obtained with his own blood."

Adam's job was to work and keep something he did not create. We function as pastors of our churches in the same way. We didn't initiate our calling or create our churches. The apostle Paul reminds us that we are merely "servants of Christ and stewards of the mysteries of God" (1 Corinthians 4:1). What is our calling as stewards? To "be found faithful" (v 2).

This would be impossible if we were not *kept* by God himself: "The LORD is your keeper; the LORD is your shade on your right hand … The LORD will keep your going out and your coming in from this time forth and forevermore" (Psalm 121:5, 8).

Remembering that God is the one who takes you, places you, and keeps you prevents ministry from becoming the pinnacle of your identity. It also helps remove that rather large anvil of performance-driven spirituality that rides so heavily on your back—the kind of spirituality that seeks applause from an audience other than God in order to be affirmed. God has put us where we are. We work for him.

Neediness Is Godliness

Notice that after God placed Adam in the garden, he didn't say, *"Adam, from this moment on you will be referred to as the groundskeeper of God—so get to work!"* No, God's first command for Adam was that he was to eat the fruit of the garden. Isn't that incredibly interesting? And lovely? (I mean, for the record, nobody has ever had to command me to eat anything. I'm super happy to do it without any prompting whatsoever.)

The Lord commanded the man to eat because Adam was a creaturely caretaker, who needed food to energize him for the work. Adam's pre-fall body required rest, nourishment, and renewal. All that working, keeping, and caretaking required physical refueling. Isn't that a wonderful thing to remember about our Creator? He commands us to eat because he created our bodies to need the food that he provides to sustain them. It says something about God's heart for humans that he made them to be needy, to know when they were hungry, and to reach out and pluck a piece of fruit from a vine so that they wouldn't grow weary and faint on the job. This doesn't stop being true when we become pastors. On a basic but profound level, God has placed us in the church to work it and keep it, while knowing our place in it—which is that of a human being who will require constant food, water, rest, and renewal.

Do you feel guilty about attending to your physical needs, pastor? Do you ignore taking a break and enjoying a good meal? Do you feel ashamed for taking a nap? Does taking a sabbath day feel self-indulgent? God gave you, as a human being, the means to address your basic bodily needs. What does it say about our opinion of God's good design if we so easily discount such means? Are we willing to face some of the negative physical effects that come with ignoring them? God forbid!

Our creaturely needs are not God's plan B; this was all God's doing before Adam had ever taken one bite of forbidden fruit. We do well to embrace them.

Created for Companionship

Adam was also created for unique companionship. As Genesis 2 continues, we learn that Adam was unable to discover another creature that could relate to him in the intricate, complex, and human way that God had created him for. What he needed was another human being. So God provided just that.

> But for Adam there was not found a helper fit for him. So the Lord God caused a deep sleep to fall upon the man, and while he slept took one of his ribs and closed up its place with flesh. And the rib that the Lord God had taken from the man he made into a woman and brought her to the man. (Genesis 2:20-22)

It wasn't a lack of effort that kept Adam from finding a suitable helper. There were plenty of creatures to name, plenty of garden varieties to tend, and no shortage of work to be done. The problem was that none of these animals or activities could fill Adam's deep spiritual and emotional need for human companionship with a flesh-and-bone image-bearer of God. Which is why the creation of Eve was not a random backup plan that God found in his discarded-ideas folder. It was another example of God making something (here, someone) for Adam that addressed his need. It leads Adam to write some joy-filled poetry:

> Then the man said, "This at last is bone of my bones and flesh of my flesh; she shall be called Woman, because she was taken out of Man." (2:23)

Eve's creation does not elevate Adam to something he is not. It grounds Adam in the person God made him to be by using his very body to create another person made in God's image.

Life-Sized Limitations

If we pay close enough attention, we can see the initial ocean-sized droplets of God's grace toward our humanity in these origin verses. We can see that God created Adam and Eve in his image as those who had physical, spiritual, and emotional limitations:

- **Physical:** They needed the food that God provided.
- **Spiritual:** They needed the words that God commanded.
- **Emotional:** They needed the companionship that God created.

By the way, if this makes Adam and Eve sound a whole lot "needier" than we ever imagined them to be, it means that we have wrongly thought of our human limits as something that happened due to *the curse* rather than *the creation*. God breathed a life of limitations into the nostrils of Adam and Eve. They couldn't work and keep the garden 24 hours per day. They couldn't name and care for the animals without lunch breaks. They couldn't manufacture their own food. They couldn't walk for days on end with God in the garden. They couldn't find their own companion nor be the only companion the other person would ever need.

All around Adam and Eve was evidence of their need, of their humanity, of their inability to breathe their next breath without the care of their loving and sovereign Creator. By design, the image of God is reflected through the limitations of our humanity—our total dependence on God for all things. After all, if you're an image-*bearer*, that means you aren't the original image. Our limits point back to the one who is limitless.

I pause here, and I read over that last paragraph I just wrote. It's a nice pastoral paragraph in a nice pastoral book on unhurriedness. But my heart has a hard time receiving it because I don't want the limitations that come with being an image-bearer to be what best reflects God's glory. I want to build something as impressive as the Tower of Babel to best reflect me… I mean, God. You see, limitations make me feel that I'm losing the potential to be all that I dream I can be. Yet Scripture tells me that this appetite for being all that I dream I can be is what Satan used as a lure in Eden to deceive my forefather. So, I need to reimagine what was lost so that it doesn't remain lost on me.

Before and After

Imagine the joy that would have existed in the hearts of Adam and Eve before their fall from perfection. Imagine the unhurried work in the garden, the slow savoring of the delicious fruit that God had grown for them, the fulfilling and companionable time they spent together under the watchful eye of their happy Creator.

All was right in the world until God was wronged by two people who wanted to be God and whose humanity was fractured in the heartbreaking aftermath. It's not as if Adam hadn't been warned.

Immediately after commanding Adam to eat the trees of the garden, God told Adam that there was a kind of fruit he was *not* to eat. A certain kind of fruit tree existed in the garden that would not nourish Adam's body but damage his soul. It was this food that would eventually be used by the serpent to tempt God's first people to become more than human, which would in turn make them less than human and lead to the death of all their human offspring.

The origin story of our fall unfolds to a soundtrack of tragedy and regret:

[The serpent] said to the woman, "Did God actually say, 'You shall not eat of any tree in the garden'?" And the

woman said to the serpent, "We may eat of the fruit of the trees in the garden, but God said, 'You shall not eat of the fruit of the tree that is in the midst of the garden, neither shall you touch it, lest you die.'" But the serpent said to the woman, "You will not surely die. For God knows that when you eat of it your eyes will be opened, and you will be like God, knowing good and evil." (Genesis 3:1-5)

Don't miss the subtlety of the serpent's question to Eve. He puts God's word to the test by asking Eve if God has really placed limitations on what they can and cannot eat. The question almost feels disorienting to Eve at first: *Of course God did not say we couldn't eat from any tree… just one tree, or we will die.* But then the serpent's response drives to the heart of all temptations: "You will not surely die." In other words, *The things you desire to do, over and above what the Lord has desired and commanded for you, will actually enhance your life.* The serpent was saying, *God wants to limit you. He made you a human being so that he could rule over you without fear of his rule being threatened. Ignore him. Become like him. Be like God.*

What's so interesting is that Adam and Eve were already, in the sense that God had purposed, *like* God. They had both and together been created in his image *with limitations*, which best reflected the beautiful union they had with their Creator. Adam and Eve's desire wasn't to be *like* God as much as it was to *be God*, and to be his equal in power, intellect, and control. They wanted to be more than human. But, in their aspiration to be God, they were immediately stripped of the greatest privilege of their humanity—eternal communion with their Creator.

As we reflect on this tragic origin story, we should be utterly confounded by the vastness of God's goodness. Although Adam and Eve would lose their perfect humanity, God had already perfected a plan as vast as the universe itself to restore it to them and to their future fallen offspring.

But what if we pause for a minute and take a hard look at the ways we attempt to be more-than-human pastors? What if we stand back and, unlike Adam, pray before reaching out to take a bite of that super bad super-fruit? What if we see the ministry in which God put us to work and keep the church as something that is meant to be done within the beautiful limitations that he has blessed us with? How might our humanity be redeemed, not so that we can be better *pastors* but so that we can be blessed *persons* who pastor as holier and therefore happier *human beings*?

We don't stand where Adam and Eve did in Genesis 3. We stand on the other side of the cross. Jesus has come. He has crushed the serpent. He has indwelled us with his Spirit. And he empowers us to once more live as the human beings we were designed to be. So let's consider how we can start to do that. As we continue, I know that words on pages are easier than deeds in practice—but there's grace for this too, as in all things.

A Happier and Holier Humanity

Offer your humanity to your leaders

Whatever your church leadership structure (elders, deacons, leadership team, etc.), one of the ways you can guard against becoming a more-than-human pastor is by offering your humanity to your fellow leaders (who, remember, happen to be human too). Remind them of your fears and frailties, your incompetence and inconsistencies, and your leanings and limitations. I wonder if they wouldn't be surprised. It may be that they perceive you as possessing levels of gifting, abilities, and capacities that exceed reality. Or it could be that your leaders have a decent handle on your strengths as a *pastor*, but to hear you express yourself to them as a *person* would open a door for them to extend greater care to you.

This will not be a one-time conversation and, in some cases, not an easy one either. Laying our humanity bare to our fellow leaders will likely surface expose complexities, because these can be tender spaces you're inviting your people to step into. And that's ok. You will have an opportunity to meet them in *their humanity* and then wonder together with them at what God might do if you all learn what it means to embrace being the people God is redeeming you all to become.

Find a friend to help you observe and embrace humanity

Friends are hard to find in our line of work, which makes it worth working hard to find some. A good friend, one who understands your vocation and the temptations that come with it, will help you see what your more-than-human tendencies obscure from your vision. A good friend will be winsomely curious, ask gracious questions, listen with intentionality, and offer sage wisdom that you can receive with gladness—and sometimes sadness, especially on the days when you realize that you have lost sight of your humanity in a haze of ministry "productivity."

Can I be honest with you? Even as I write this, I feel grief well up within me over my astounding lack of the kind of friends I'm describing. In some seasons, we wander through life and ministry feeling utterly alone. We are like Elijah when he found himself in the middle of nowhere after his victory on Mount Carmel, trying to escape from the evil clutches of Queen Jezebel (1 Kings 19). Most of our lives aren't quite as dramatic as his, but we do identify with the kind of loneliness-drenched fatigue that Elijah experienced, until God stepped in, stopped him in his tracks, and soothed his angst.

How do I find these kind of friends, Ronnie? If I had a clear answer to that, I'd write a best-selling book called *How to*

Find Good Friends. But since I'm not that good, or God, all I can say is that, like every lack in your life, you address it by expressing your longing to God. Then see what kind of people he might bring your way; or he might reveal a person that's already there. God happens to know that you are a person who needs people to help you become the person he has created you to be. You know what else? He will give you grace during the wilderness years. Scripture overflows with proof that this is true.

Pray that God would continue to sanctify your humanity

Since I just mentioned prayer, let's double down on that for a moment. Grasping our humanity comes as the result of growing in humility, and humility is forged through prayer.

We'll come back to the idea of humility in the next chapter. For now, though, consider this prayer of David: "O Lord, make me know my end and what is the measure of my days; let me know how fleeting I am!" (Psalm 39:4). As is often the case, he is singing a chorus full of minor chords, pleading with God to help him grasp his fragile humanity. David goes on: "Surely all mankind stands as a mere breath! Surely a man goes about as a shadow!" (v 5-6).

As a pastor who finds it easy to fool himself, these verses from David's songbook remind me that honest prayers laid at the feet of God will keep me grounded and guarded. This puts me in a horrible but great predicament. Horrible because the humility that comes through honest prayer will bring with it painful revelations—constantly reminding me of how I'm becoming less than human, as I default time and time again to striving to become more than human. But also great because, well, read that last sentence again.

Through prayer and in community, God is making us more and more like the *persons* he desires to *pastor* his church. His sanctifying work gives us back our humanity. And our joy.

CHAPTER TWO

Humility

*"*Who said I was humble?"

I was sitting about five feet (1.5m) from the stage when John Piper made this comment to a small group of pastors in an upstairs bar that was doubling as a pre-conference venue for an event I was attending. You read that right; I said upstairs *bar*. Let's stay focused.

I remember thinking to myself, "I wonder if these high-profile pastors actually struggle with humility?"

It took all of 3 seconds for my low-profile pastor brain to realize that if I struggle with humility to the degree that I do, how much more for someone who has a veritable army of seminary fanboys, theology nerds, and legions of everyday pastors reading their books, liking their tweets, and gobbling up their every word like Cookie Monster at a Nabisco factory?

Humility is a funny thing—and by funny I mean one of the least funny things to invade a pastor's heart. The thing about humility is that it's inextricably linked to our humanity. Revisiting our journey back to Eden from chapter 1, we see that Adam's desire to be more than human was fueled by pride. As Tim Keller is quoted as saying, "Pride is that which claims to be the author of what is really a gift."

If we desire an unhurried ministry, we need to have a serious internal counseling session with ourselves (or with a genuine counselor) to assess how our relationship with humility is coming along. Humility will only come to fruition alongside humanity, as its sought-after companion.

Now, I don't know that I've ever typed a sentence that fills me with greater feelings of fear and hypocrisy than that last one, and that's because, on my best days, I know who I really am.

I am not a humble man.

The problem with that statement is that the speaker can look real good when they make a claim like that. Even typing that short sentence triggered a subtle but all-too-smug satisfaction in my heart as I envisioned you hearing me admit that painful but hardly shocking revelation. Faux-humility (ok, faux-*anything*) not only fools congregations, but it also fools pastors themselves, giving them license to recklessly career down perilous back roads that look like safe highways to everyone else. The problem with asking, "Who said I was humble?" is that you can probably answer back with "A lot of people, actually." The fact that our congregations can be fooled means that we are also likely fooling ourselves.

And yet…

By God's grace I am "being transformed into the same image from one degree of glory to another" (2 Corinthians 3:18). I'm stunned when I remember that Jesus is still doing the work of transforming my faux everything into faithful everything, so that my life becomes a more authentic and humble representation of everything he is.

I know this almost feels like the end of a mercifully short chapter, but there's more to be said. Let's spend some time talking about how humility contributes to the unhurried life that we long for as *persons* who *pastor* God's flock.

Pastoral or Prideful Life?

By nature, pastoral life is one that tempts us toward a prideful life.

You would think it was the opposite, huh? For the most part, when people envision a pastor, they think of someone who makes it their "ambition to lead a quiet life" (1 Thessalonians 4:11, NIV), eagerly shepherds the flock of God (1 Peter 5:2), and preaches the word with complete patience and teaching (2 Timothy 4:2). This is how we traditionally imagine the spirit of a pastor—not because we have created some unrealistic vision of ministry, but because Scripture has laid it out for us like that. People can (and should) think of pastors as those who speak gently, carry a well-read Bible, provide nuggets of wisdom, and always have a listening ear available for anyone willing to share their sorrows. For their part, many pastors do their best to uphold this public image to parishioners.

But I wonder if a different kind of pastoral life is being offered to pastors like us today? One that has been hijacked by success-driven strategists, edgy entrepreneurs, and leadership-seminar gurus who tempt pastors to reinvent the pastoral life into something that can be measured on an Excel spreadsheet.

Ironically, pastors don't even need this kind of "help" for their life to become more prideful than pastoral. There's a constant temptation to try to be in control, like God—a temptation which transcends time and culture. Yet this additional, 21st-century temptation for pastoral ministry to morph into something it was never intended to be is everywhere, and in its wake are frustrated, disillusioned, worn-out pastors who attempt to measure their effectiveness with metrics that only work in places where the care of souls is not necessary.

This pride can flesh itself out in two specific ways (among others). Depending on the person and their life experiences, pride can have a pastor believing that everything they touch turns to gold because they have bought into the mindset that they are the ones with the power and charisma to control the destiny of their churches and ministries. What makes this even more troubling is that this kind of leader is usually applauded and affirmed for exhibiting this style of leadership behavior.

The flipside to this is the pastor with an inverted sense of pride. They compare themselves with the successful and (over)confident pastors of the world, and only measure their effectiveness by the accomplishments that everybody can see. Such pastors may appear more humble on the outside but are likely just as self-focused as the more overtly prideful pastors. Both have put themselves in the center of a calling that is inherently *not about them* and have adopted a heart posture that keeps their eyes firmly stuck on "me."

These are broken metrics.

And here's a thought—do pastors need "metrics?"

If you're reading this book as someone who's been a pastor for a while, you may have some on-the-job experience of all the ways in which a pastor is tempted to do almost anything but, well, *pastor*: that is, pursuing personal holiness, cultivating a devoted prayer life, caring for your people, and preaching the word. The problem is that I'm *not ok* with just doing those things because I fear that *my people* are not ok with me just doing those things. Eugene Peterson wasn't wrong when he said that nobody knows what a pastor does on the other six days of the week. So what ends up happening is that I invest my time in opportunities that *increase my visibility*. I move beyond my calling in order to position myself as a *relentless doer* rather than a *receiver*. Instead of pursuing the (largely unseen) practices of communion with Jesus, formation in his word, and relational cultivation with his people, I treat my role as more like that of a general contractor—making sure everyone can see what I'm building and affirm my progress—

without giving the slightest attention to the state of my soul or the well-being of my body.

But this is all kinds of folly. As with a gardener that greets their plants and flowers with a water pail on a warm summer morning, your care for your body and soul helps you *become* the person you're called to *be*, before you spend even an hour doing the work of the *pastor* that people expect you to be. I kind of think you should read that last sentence more than once, if you wouldn't mind.

When a pastor considers humility to be one of their life pursuits, there will be an emphasis on the word *be* over the word *do*. Make no mistake, *doing* is essential, but *doing* in the absence of *becoming* is how I become *undone* as a pastor.

This presents us with a tension though. I remember trying to flesh this out to a group of men at a gathering for church planters, after which one came up to me and said something along the lines of "I hear what you're saying, but all of this talk of *being* over *doing* is frustrating to me. What am I supposed to do? Just sit around and do nothing so that I can be something?"

Well, not exactly. James makes it clear that we are to be *doers* of the word so that we don't deceive ourselves into thinking we are something that we are not:

> But be doers of the word, and not hearers only, deceiving yourselves. For if anyone is a hearer of the word and not a doer, he is like a man who looks intently at his natural face in a mirror. For he looks at himself and goes away and at once forgets what he was like. But the one who looks into the perfect law, the law of liberty, and perseveres, being no hearer who forgets but a doer who acts, he will be blessed in his doing. (James 1:22-25)

Yet I think it's fairly significant that James mentions *looking* into the perfect law of liberty—embodied in the person of

Jesus—so that we can be a "doer who acts." This clues us in that James was not simply talking about the work of our hands but the work of our heart. We have to "hear" before we can "do" and "look" before we can "act."

So let's look at Jesus now and ask, "How do we cultivate a humble, unhurried heart?"

Unhurried Heart

The story of Mary and Martha illustrates how a good grasp on our limitations will help cultivate a heart for Jesus—showing us how to make godly distinctions between the portions of our life that can be helps or hindrances to deeper discipleship with Jesus. In Luke 10:38-42, two familiar domestic scenes unfold:

> Now as they went on their way, Jesus entered a village. And a woman named Martha welcomed him into her house. And she had a sister called Mary, who sat at the Lord's feet and listened to his teaching. But Martha was distracted with much serving. And she went up to him and said, "Lord, do you not care that my sister has left me to serve alone? Tell her then to help me." But the Lord answered her, "Martha, Martha, you are anxious and troubled about many things, but one thing is necessary. Mary has chosen the good portion, which will not be taken away from her."

The first scene that unfolds focuses on Mary, who, upon Jesus' arrival, immediately drops everything she is doing, pulls up a beanbag, and sits at his feet to hear his teaching. Mary is not letting the opportunity to listen to Jesus pass her by. Imagine hosting a famous musician at your house and having the opportunity to sit down in the living room and hear them play all of your favorite songs.

Jesus commends her and says that Mary has chosen the "one thing" necessary. Yet for Mary to choose this one thing meant that she had to choose not to be occupied with another thing. To sit at Jesus' feet meant she had to quite literally *get off her own feet*, embrace that she couldn't do two things at once, and decide to do what would be most spiritually profitable for her soul. Notice too that Jesus never feels the need to warn Mary about guarding against laziness or idleness, and that is because time spent with Jesus seems to be the greatest guard *against* laziness and idleness.[8] Jesus has a counterintuitive approach to productivity that puts the work of the heart before the work of the hands—while not denigrating the work of the hands because, after all, he created humans to be productive with their hands.

Luke is keen on pointing out the wisdom-soaked humility of Mary: she recognizes the invitation of the Lord and receives him, even though in this culture her being a woman would have usually relegated her to a role of serving over learning.[9] Mary provides sage insight for our pastoral souls. She understood that Jesus was offering something more nourishing to her soul than anything that could be gained by any food she might have served to Jesus and his disciples. When she had the opportunity, Mary wisely consumed the spiritual food of Jesus.[10]

You would think it should be the opposite, but we pastors have an incredibly difficult time receiving the meal that Jesus offers to us in his word, even though we are constantly encouraging others to partake of it as much as possible. This is where we need humility to recognize not only that we need the food of Jesus' word as much as our people but that we need to receive and partake of it *all the more*. In the dizzying push and pull of pastoral life, coming under the constant instruction of God's word is the way in which our hearts will remain pliable toward God and God's people.

Why is it so hard for us to receive Jesus as Mary did? Perhaps it's because receiving puts us in a posture of repose, not activity, like a boxer who gets massaged and taped up before a fight. We just want to get in there already. Yet it would be ridiculous for a boxer to run to the ring without receiving the preparation his body needs to engage in the battle that's about to begin.

I wonder if it would help us to think about Mary when our eagerness to rush into the activity of ministry drives us to run out the door in the morning way too soon. Jesus *praises* Mary because she chose "the good portion." I'm no theological genius, but it seems to me that this tells us something about what Jesus considers most valuable to himself—and best for us.

Hurried Hands

As Mary sits at the feet of Jesus, Martha is described as being "distracted" by the amount of serving to be done, which results in her excessive level of anxiety. Again, Jesus never denigrates the act of serving. Serving one another is highlighted in the New Testament as evidence that the love of God is genuine in a person, whether it's serving through sacrificial love (Galatians 5:13), or as an act of worship (Luke 7:36-38). Martha's serving was rebuked by Jesus because it had become a narcissistic form of hospitality that was in conflict with the growth and expression of her faith.[11] The argument here is that Martha "chose" the work of her *hands* over the work of her *heart*, even though the opportunity had been given to prioritize the latter with absolutely no hint that she would need to give up the former.

Martha asks Jesus, "Lord, do you not care that my sister has left me to serve alone? Tell her then to help me" (Luke 10:40). The tone of Martha's complaint to Jesus clearly illustrates how hurried activity can lead to anxiety and agitation.[12] Her accusatory words show how easy it is to mischaracterize Jesus when a desire to be near him has become less important.[13]

Not only does Martha mischaracterize Jesus, but she also mischaracterizes Mary's motives! She believes that her sister's decision to sit at Jesus' feet means that the level of hospitality they provide for their guest will be unsatisfactory.

I am filled with sadness when I think of pastors, like myself, running Martha-like marathons, trying to make sure everyone affirms our worth as God's most accomplished servant. Yet a preoccupation with our occupation doesn't end in Jesus heaping words of praise on our heads. If our busyness with the practical side of ministry seduces us from giving wholehearted attention to the things of God, it instead draws Jesus' correction.[14]

Luke is showing us that we first need to *be* like Mary and then we can *do* what Martha does with renewed and unhurried hearts. By becoming "busy" with the "good portion" of listening to Jesus, we can cultivate an "unbusy heart" for the other areas God has given us to serve in for the sake of the kingdom.

As the pressures of ministry life beckon pastors to become productivity machines and replace the good portion of Jesus with more measurable activities, pastors can take good counsel from the posture of Mary and the kind rebuke given to Martha. The truth is that every pastor is in danger of becoming anxious with many ministry things, but it is also true that the grace of Christ will guard every pastor from being characterized by busyness and anxiety when they sit at his feet with hearts ready to receive. Otherwise, pastors will look in the mirror one day and see a person that does not resemble a shepherd anymore.

Being Served by Jesus

As a pastor who longs for the unhurried life, I need to see my human limits as a gift that leads me to a place of humility before the Lord—looking to be served by him—rather than my starting point always being how I can serve him. Pastors who are served by Jesus are the ones who best serve Jesus.

The Psalms are such a help for us as we seek to become more like Christ in how we *do* ministry. Can I offer some simple encouragement, as someone who undoubtedly needs more help with this than you?

Adjust your vision

> O LORD, *my heart is not lifted up; my eyes are not raised too high; I do not occupy myself with things too great and too marvelous for me. But I have calmed and quieted my soul, like a weaned child with its mother; like a weaned child is my soul within me. (Psalm 131:1-2)*

Psalm 131 is a beautiful picture of one whose soul finds contentment in the comfort of Jesus' care. But the first part of the passage is interesting for pastors because we have the tendency to occupy ourselves with things that may be "too great and too marvelous" for us. This might be a good desire to see many people come to Christ, a good aspiration to see your church become a change agent in your community, or a good concern for your people becoming distracted by worldly cares. These are all great and marvelous things—but they ultimately rest in the Lord's hands, not ours.

Notice how the psalmist speaks to the Lord. He tells the Lord what he is doing with his eyes. He acknowledges that, yes, there are great and marvelous things out there to see and ponder, but they are not for him to become hurried with. Instead, like Mary, he's content to simply be close to God.

Did the psalmist have some magic potion that helped him calm and quiet his soul? Something delicious to drink? A new series on Netflix? His favorite meal? A vacation on the coast of Italy? No, the psalmist calms and quiets his soul "like a weaned child"—as one whose perspective has been sanctified through the trials of being "weaned" off the elementary cravings and desires that marked his immaturity (v 2).

As pastors, we need to continually adjust our vision by resetting our gaze on the Shepherd of our souls. This is how we embrace our humanity. This is how we can pastor with calm and quiet souls. Imagine the effectiveness of a congregation that has a pastor who spends their time calming and quieting their souls with Jesus?

Lower your eyes, for this is where stillness resides.

Wave a white flag

> *I will instruct you and teach you in the way you should go;*
> *I will counsel you with my eye upon you.*
> *Be not like a horse or a mule, without understanding,*
> *which must be curbed with bit and bridle,*
> *or it will not stay near you.*
> *Many are the sorrows of the wicked,*
> *but steadfast love surrounds*
> *the one who trusts in the LORD. (Psalm 32:8-10)*

I remember when my daughter was a baby (just learning to walk), and I would sometimes need to hold her when she didn't want to be held. She would do this rather masterful squirming motion by which she could slip down through my arms and run off to freedom... or death—especially if I was holding her on a crowded street. (Come to think of it, my cat has that same maneuver.)

What was so infuriating about that pro-level baby move was that the best place for her to be at that moment was in my arms. There was a *reason* why I was holding her. I was trying to protect her or teach her something that required her to be held firmly in my grasp to understand. She didn't have the maturity to humble herself in the love and safety of her papa's arms.

As pastors, we too sometimes fight the Lord's nurturing of us. We're like toddlers who must be restrained with a firm grasp—or, as the psalmist puts it, like mules who must be controlled with the pull of a bit and a bridle. We have places to go to, things to see, people to help, sermons to craft, platforms to build, and the list goes on. But the psalm's wise words are saying, *Don't be like this! Don't be someone who refuses to learn.* Instead, we pastors need to *wave the white flag.* We need to surrender our stubborn wills and infantile immaturities. We need to see how God is moving in our life and slip into his jetstream so that his direction becomes the course of our lives.

Let me give you an example from my own life as a pastor.

I am someone who gets excited about building new things. Happily, the building our church owns used to be an old furniture warehouse—which means that over the years I've had opportunity to embark all kinds of great and marvelous projects to improve it. Yet what I've found over the years is that not everyone is like me. Not everyone feels that being in a constant state of improving the warehouse is the best direction for the church. The problem is that making these improvements gives me a sense of progress and accomplishment that I can become all-too-easily addicted to. I've had to learn to slow down, choose the best time to suggest new building projects, and not stomp my feet like an impatient child, when other leaders either don't catch the vision or think we should simply wait.

For me to discern God's direction requires unhurried listening and learning. It requires me to daily surrender to the settled and steadfast love of God, who will do what he feels is necessary to keep me from the danger of my desires. Ultimately, this requires humility.

Humility is the clarion call for the hurried pastor. Why?

It slows us down so that we can receive instruction for where we should go, and how we should get there.

It keeps our hearts in tune with the heart of Christ so that we can better sense his presence when life and ministry become overwhelmingly busy and chaotic.

It creates greater self-awareness by casting a spotlight on the condition of our heart while guarding us against self-condemnation.

Humility makes us more like Jesus, who shepherds us as we become shepherds like him.

The beauty of a humble life is that it always has joy in its sights! Humility does not deprive us of what we could have; instead, it actually delivers all that God has promised to those who sit at the feet of Jesus and lean in close.

CHAPTER THREE

Hopefulness

This is a tricky one.

When we talk about hopefulness in the life of a pastor, it seems so obvious on one hand. We expect phrases like "Look to Christ in all things," "Seek your joy in his salvation," "Don't put your trust in the things of this world," and "Be encouraged by the faithfulness of God." All of these hopeful words are good, right, and true.

But hopefulness is also a bit more complex than that, isn't it? Throwing a box of laundry detergent at dirty clothes isn't going to clean them. The detergent needs to work itself through the clothing to be effective. In a similar way, hopefulness needs to permeate the whole life of the pastor—and is key to an unhurried ministry among God's people.

Of course, no pastor would say that they have no concern about whether they are a hopeful person or not. The more revealing truth is that hopefulness is really the default setting of the human heart. We are always looking for the next thing that will satisfy our longings and desires. We could go as far to say that as human beings, we find it impossible to *not* hope for the best possible scenario to play out in our lives—and as pastors, in our ministries. Even when we are being cynical, for example, is it not just a defense mechanism against being disappointed, in case our hopes don't come to fruition? In that sense, hope is like Peter Pan's shadow. It is inescapable.

But as Christians, we know that we're meant to hope for something better than positive health outcomes or a restful vacation; we're called to set our hearts on spiritual realities that are currently far from view. Looking to embody *that* kind of hopefulness can feel like grasping for wind, even though we know it is supposed to be one of the characteristics of our faith. We actually get a taste of this relationship between hope and faith from Scripture. The book of Hebrews says that "faith is the assurance of things hoped for, the conviction of things not seen" (11:1). Paul tells us in Romans that "hope that is seen is not hope. For who hopes for what he sees? But if we hope for what we do not see, we wait for it with patience" (8:24-25).

So, there is an elusive quality to hope in some respects, because, for there to be hope, there needs to be something unseen to be *hoped for.* Yet our intrinsic propensity for hope makes hope something we will always return to. So let's make sure we're hoping for the right things. In its essence, hopeful is something Christians must *be* and increasingly *become,* because a perpetually hopeless Christian, or a perpetually hopeless pastor, has to be considered antithetical to the gospel message. Notice I used the word *perpetually* there, because every Christian stares down the long corridor of hopelessness at times and is no less God's son or daughter for doing so. What we want to explore in this chapter is how hopefulness helps us *become* and then *be* unhurried pastors who have embraced their humanity with the humility of Jesus.

The Art of Hopefulness

One of the most beautiful lines in cinematic history comes at the end of *The Shawshank Redemption.* The film tells the story of Andy and Red, who become best friends after Andy (played by Tim Robbins) is unjustly accused of murdering his wife and gets sent to prison, where he meets a "lifer" named Red (played by Morgan Freeman). Eventually, Andy hatches an elaborate escape plan that succeeds wonderfully, after which he journeys to a secluded hideaway on the coast. In time, Red gets released from prison, but he's been incarcerated for so long that the prospect of rebuilding a normal life in society feels too daunting. He comes to a critical juncture where it seems that his only choices are either to end his life or break his parole and search for Andy, who left him instructions on where to find him if the time ever came. He goes with the latter. As Red makes his decision to look for Andy instead of ending his life, these words emanate from the screen:

> I hope to see my friend and shake his hand. I hope the
> Pacific is as blue as it has been in my dreams. I hope.

The end of the film shows old Red walking down the coast to reunite with Andy, who greets him with a surprised and beautiful embrace as the end credits begin to roll.

Hope was something that inspired Red to pursue what he could not see. He didn't have a photograph of the place he was going to, but he had never forgotten Andy's face. And it was the hope of reuniting with his friend that enabled him to risk his life instead of taking his life: to take thoughtful and courageous action to pursue his greatest flourishing.

Pastors would do well to understand hopefulness in the way Red did. Whatever depth of brokenness or burdens you are experiencing in your ministry right now that make it feel like a life sentence, seeking the face of God will be the best way to persevere in hope. It will help to you move forward with greater thoughtfulness while becoming more courageous and less risk-averse.

Look at the way David the psalmist writes these desperately hopeful words from the depths of his heartbreak:

Hear, O LORD, when I cry aloud;
  be gracious to me and answer me!
You have said, "Seek my face."
My heart says to you,
  "Your face, LORD, do I seek." (Psalm 27:7-8)

When we read the Psalms, David always seems to be in a world of worry and upheaval. It isn't because he was a guy who tended to be overly emotional and prone to drama (ok, he might have been a *little bit*). It's because he regularly faced very real life-and-death situations that he had no power to manage on his own, even though he was one of the most powerful men in the world. The Psalms show David straining to keep his eyes focused on the object of his hope.

If you want to embody hopefulness, understand this: hope is something we experience more of, the more ardently we pursue the embodiment of all hope—God himself. Hope requires an unseen object for us to reset our gaze upon and to seek out with all of our hearts. Like David, we can't yet see an end to our difficulties, but we walk in faith, placing our feeble trust in the one who is sovereign over the means and the ends.

For hopefulness to be the posture of the pastor seeking the unhurried life, we must learn the art of waiting for the Lord. Look at how David wraps up his song:

I believe that I shall look upon the goodness of the LORD
  in the land of the living!
Wait for the LORD;
  be strong, and let your heart take courage;
  wait for the LORD! (v 13-14).

What do we imagine David is waiting for exactly? What are *we* waiting for? On one hand, we know how we would prefer to see God act, but waiting is an acknowledgment that we expect God to "do far more abundantly than all that we ask or think, according to the power at work within us" (Ephesians 3:20). Waiting is putting a pause on our stirring, without pausing our belief that God will not fail to deliver his goodness to us!

David *believed*, meaning David was *hopeful* that someday he would see the fulfillment of God's beautifully unbroken promises—but he also acknowledged that in order for those promises to be believed and hoped for, they must also be *waited* for.

There it is. The dreaded *W* word. I describe waiting as *dreaded* because it's not something most of us get hyped about. Waiting feels risky: not because God may or may not be in control of your life during the waiting but because relinquishing our wills to his while we wait is accepting that whatever he bestows upon us is the *better* thing.

Sandra McCracken writes in her song "Sweet Comfort":

Whatever my God ordains is right
His holy will abides
I will be still whatever he does
And follow where he guides.

That can be a cheerful song to *sing out* but a challenging one to *live out*. As I write these words, I want to grow in the kind of courageous hope that David demonstrates. But, deep down, I don't want that hopefulness to grow through waiting; I want it to be formed immediately through receiving exactly what I want, when I want. The problem is that constantly pursuing immediate gratification creates a harried life, not a hopeful one. And without waiting, there's no need for courage. This gets at the root of our hopefulness dilemma: if I know that waiting is the method God uses to infuse me with patient, courageous hope, *am I willing to wait?*

The Fruit of Hope

One of the incredible things about Amazon Prime is how lightning fast we get our packages delivered. Even as I'm writing this, a new study Bible I ordered yesterday just dropped on my porch with a healthy thump, courtesy of a Fed-Ex driver. That's what I love so much about Amazon Prime. I didn't even have to wait 24 hours for my order to show up, and all I had to do was point and click. I love that the need to wait for something I want has practically been eliminated by a person in a white truck who makes a pleasing thump on my doorstep.

When it comes to the deep and abiding work of God in our spiritual life, though, there is no Amazon Prime. We have to wait. And as we wait, we have the opportunity to cultivate the fruit of patience.

When I was growing up, Christmas Eve was one of my favorite days of the year. I mean, it still is. What I love so much about Christmas Eve is that it gets us right to the peak of our excitement for the big day, without it being the big day. It contains all of the Christmassy elements that I love so much at Christmas (food, family, carols, presents, chestnuts roasting on an open fire… ok, I'll stop) but with the added hopefulness that Christmas is *still coming*! All the mysteries, longings, and desires are still thick in the air, and mingle together to form my anticipation for my favorite day of the year.

Here's my point: as a child, my hope was so overflowing on Christmas Eve that nothing in the universe had the power to dampen my spirits or short-circuit my patience. My parents could have asked me to do the most laborious and mundane chores in the world, and I would have acted as if they were giving me an early Christmas present.

"So, if I'm looking at this list correctly, Dad, you want me to clean the whole house, weed the backyard, detail your truck, and then finish all of my homework for the entire month of

January. No problem. Let me knock out this list, and I'll pour you another cup of eggnog, pal."

The reason for this overflowing fountain of patience, even in the face of a mountain of chores?

Hopefulness.

My heart and mind were so captivated by the imminent joy waiting for me at the stroke of midnight that an almost supernatural level of patience was deposited into my soul every 24th of December. For one day in the calendar year, I was simultaneously the most hopeful and therefore most patient boy on Planet Earth. Interestingly, this hope-infused patience also kept me from being a frantic, hurried mess because I wanted to enjoy the anticipation. I reveled in every part of December 24th.

Seen like this, hope fuels patience—and patience enables us to take each day one step at a time.

Warring against Hopelessness

Some days, we feel like we're pastoring on December 24th. But then there are the other days. The days that feel more like January 17th. And let's face it: these days are far more common. It's difficult to grasp hope-infused patience in the midst of the murderously mundane aspects of pastoring.

Pastors are typically waging war with feelings of hopelessness. Hopelessness can be the result of so many things: details of our life that leave us disillusioned, depressed, and in denial of God's goodness.

Maybe you find yourself in a church that turned out to not be the greatest fit for you and your family, and you currently don't see any other options. Or perhaps there's a relationship with an elder, staff worker, or church member that remains filled with tension despite your best efforts to establish peace. Maybe you're frustrated that despite your zealous prayers and relentless activity, your church hasn't seen any growth, and your members seem to have lost commitment. You might be in a place where you feel exhausted both physically and emotionally, and you don't see any way to regain your strength.

In these situations, what are the first steps back to hope?

Elijah helps us here.

1 Kings 18 – 19 is the story of a man who sank into the deep quagmire of hopelessness and needed the persistent heart of God to provide him with practical and spiritual encouragement in order to continue in his prophetic calling.

This particular part of Elijah's story begins with a ministry victory like no other: a head-to-head epic showdown with the prophets of Baal.

I'm guessing you know the story: Elijah challenges the false prophets of Israel to a contest to determine who was the true and living god—Baal or Yahweh. With a flourish of pyrotechnics, the Lord answers Elijah decisively, the people fall on their faces in worship, and the false prophets' reign of terror comes to a humiliating and perilous end. I can only imagine the emotions that Elijah must have been experiencing at this moment. The contest could have gone so wrong, but the Lord responded promptly to the prayer of his pleading servant and revealed his power among his people once again.

Obviously, most of us don't experience ministry "victories" in quite as dramatic a fashion as this one. For us, it can be an unbeliever who repents and believes the gospel, a church member who is finally healed of a long-standing disease or addiction, a relational reconciliation, or a financial need that finally gets met. These are not insignificant answers to prayers. We rejoice like crazy, while being reminded of the Lord's faithfulness and provision. I'm taken aback when I think of how kind the Lord is in providing these bright evidences of his grace. They serve as beacons of hope when the darkness falls.

Because eventually, the darkness does fall, as it did with Elijah. As we near the end of chapter 18, the Lord ends the drought in Israel by providing a miraculous rainstorm. The supernatural stuff continues as God grants Elijah the legs of Usain Bolt to outrun King Ahab in his chariot as they make their way to Jezreel, where the wicked Queen Jezebel is waiting. Of course, she's not happy after learning that Elijah wiped out her entire squad of prophets, so she vows at the beginning of chapter 19 to end Elijah's life.

Now, it's no small thing when the most powerful woman in the nation vows to take your life in the next 24 hours. I can imagine not being incredibly hungry that night when it was time to sit down for dinner. Elijah can't appeal to county law officials, write a letter to his district superintendent, or call an emergency elders meeting. The only thing he can think to do in his panic is to flee to Beersheba with his servant and then take a hike into the wilderness to get some distance from everyone in his life, good or bad. This is where the story of Elijah's war against hopelessness begins.

But he himself went a day's journey into the wilderness and came and sat down under a broom tree. And he asked that he might die, saying, "It is enough; now, O LORD, take away my life, for I am no better than my fathers." And he lay down and slept under a broom tree. And behold, an angel touched him and said to him, "Arise and eat." And he looked, and behold, there was at his head a cake baked on hot stones and a jar of water. And he ate and drank and lay down again. And the angel of the LORD came again a second time and touched him and said, "Arise and eat, for the journey is too great for you." And he arose and ate and drank, and went in the strength of that food forty days and forty nights to Horeb, the mount of God. (1 Kings 19:4-8)

Elijah has sunk into a deep, deep depression, to the point that he asks the Lord to take his life. He's just come off a great victory for the Lord, but he sees himself as like his fathers before him, whose prophetic voices calling the people to follow God were met with deaf ears.

How often do we feel this way? We prepare faithful sermons, listen to the hurting, pray for the sick, encourage the downcast, and comfort the weak, and sometimes all we're met with are people who want to criticize us or, worse yet, see us taken down or removed altogether for no justifiable reason.

For the first time in who knows how long, Elijah arrives at an *unhurried place*. He is downcast, and he is depleted, but he also has *time* to be honest before the Lord. Elijah's prayer echoes many of the psalms in how it doesn't try to qualify or sanitize the groanings of his heart. *I don't want to live anymore; it's hopeless to keep going on like this*, Elijah prays.

Yet look at how God responds. He doesn't give Elijah a sermon, reminding him of all the ways he has moved on Elijah's behalf and pointing out that if he would just trust the Lord, everything would be all right. Although that's TRUE, it's not how God responds. What he does do is to provide Elijah with the essentials: food and rest. Elijah lies down in his exhaustion and just sleeps. Eventually, an angel wakes him and gives him food and water, and then... there's more sleep. He wakes again and replenishes himself with enough food and water to last the next 40 days' travel to Horeb.

We would do well to not miss the significance of replenishing our body and soul with food and rest. The Lord cares about you as the holistic being he created you to be. The first step in our war against hopelessness is sometimes just stopping and caring for our bodies with the simple means that the Lord has given us to care for them: food and rest. Why do we dismiss so easily what God made so valuable for the health and welfare of our being? Pastors can view food and rest as less important transitions to the "real work" they are called to and then find themselves in places of spiritual, emotional, and physical depletion as a result. Although our battle against hopelessness will likely consist of *more* than simply pursuing food and rest, we will not win this war without giving good and godly attention to these fundamentals, which come from the good hand of God himself.

Abounding In Hope

So, having attended to the fundamentals, what next? As we make our way further down chapter 19, we see God having a conversation with Elijah. It quickly becomes clear that the prophet's hopelessness has turned into acute bitterness:

> *There he came to a cave and lodged in it. And behold, the word of the LORD came to him, and he said to him, "What are you doing here, Elijah?" He said, "I have been very jealous for the LORD, the God of hosts. For the people of Israel have forsaken your covenant, thrown down your altars, and killed your prophets with the sword, and I, even I only, am left, and they seek my life, to take it away."*
> (v 9-10)

Self-pity has taken hold of Elijah's heart, and he's lost all sense of perspective—which is what self-pity has the tendency to do to us. He lists all the things that he has done for God and comes to the conclusion that he's the only man left on earth who is still faithful. Can you relate? As pastors, we can get to hopeless places where it feels that nobody is left, and we are the last remaining remnant of God's faithful people. Writing it out like this feels ridiculous, but I have had moments like this, and I've listened to countless pastors battling the same emotions.

It's important in these moments to ask ourselves the same question God asks Elijah: "What are you doing here?" In other words, don't just sink into the mire of bitterness and self-pity; ask yourself why you are in this place. Recount the events that have led to where you are and consider what the Lord has done, and what he is doing. We war against hopelessness by slowing down to hear the low whisper of God reassure us:

> *And [God] said, "Go out and stand on the mount before the LORD." And behold, the LORD passed by, and a great and strong wind tore the mountains and broke in pieces the rocks before the LORD, but the LORD was not in the wind. And after the wind an earthquake, but the LORD was not in the earthquake. And after the earthquake a fire, but the LORD was not in the fire. And after the fire the sound of a low whisper. (v 11-12)*

It's interesting that the Lord provides Elijah with wind, an earthquake, and fire before speaking to him in "the sound of a low whisper" (v 12b). We don't know what God actually says to Elijah until he commands him to "Go, return on your way to the wilderness of Damascus" (v 15a). But we do know that the Lord worked in the desolate wilderness moments of Elijah's life to bring him back to a place of hopefulness and send him out once more into his prophetic ministry. God doesn't use a lot of words here but demonstrates his love and care to Elijah through food, rest, nature, and low whispers.

This is how God leads hopeless, hurried pastors to abound once again in unhurried hope. What we see in the story of Elijah is a man who served God well but needed to be served by God even more. Does this feel like something you need today? To enter into a place of unhurriedness so that God can provide for your physical needs of food and rest, as well as your spiritual needs of reassurance and encouragement? What does it look like for you, in your unique context, to step into the hope that God has given you in Jesus?

It may be that you need to surrender to some time in the wilderness like Elijah, knowing that you will be in a place to hear God's voice speak to you. Perhaps you need to be honest with God about some aspects of your life that are inhibiting your hope—or ways in which you've been running to easy answers to questions when you need to give God time to answer them. Maybe you'd find it helpful to make a list of all the ways in which God has preserved you through a difficult season so that you have a physical reminder of why hoping in him has not been an exercise in futility after all!

What is stopping you from stopping everything in order to pursue the kind of hope that God promises to give his people but which you need unhurried time to receive?

I'll stop right here so that you can stop right there.

Part 2

Power

By Ronnie Martin

CHAPTER FOUR

Self-Awareness

I wasn't sure how to begin this chapter.

So let me start here: as I've matured spiritually, I've grown increasingly aware of my own lack of self-awareness. I don't think that's an oxymoron. Embarrassingly, one of the things I used to pride myself on was my (self-proclaimed) abundance of self-awareness. Of course, only someone who was lacking an abundance of self-awareness would pride themselves on their abundance of it.

In some ways, we are all engaged in a spiritual battle to become more self-aware, in a whole host of areas. We need to be self-aware not just in regard to our sin and shortcomings but also the deep-seated wounds that nestle in the hidden places of our hearts. And on the flip side, self-awareness is also about knowing our unique blend of talents and gifts, as well as the things in this world that give us liveliness and joy.

Granted, self-awareness is a *mountain* of a topic to address in one chapter of a book on unhurried pastoral ministry. So what I will attempt to do is explore how self-awareness relates to our *limitations*.

To do that, let me begin with someone a bit less limited than me in a bunch of areas. The 16th-century Reformer John Calvin wrote, "Nearly all the wisdom we possess, that is to say, true and sound wisdom, consists in two parts: the knowledge of God and of ourselves…"[15] What Calvin was driving at, in this opening line of his classic *Institutes of the Christian Religion*, is that wisdom—which is the application of what is right and true—is only possible when one has a growing awareness of *who God is* and *who we are* in light of that knowledge. In other words, without a growing understanding of things such as the glorious attributes of God, our origins as God's created image-bearers, and the depth of our sin due to the fall (to name just a few), we will be impaired in our spiritual vision.

I remember the day my older sister came home with her first set of eyeglasses. I love my sis, but this girl has not been blessed with particularly awesome eyesight. What I've never forgotten is the way she described the world after she put on those prescription glasses. She marveled at how bright, colorful, and clear everything around her was, as if she was seeing all the details of the world for the very first time in her life. Of course, she could still *see* before she got her glasses, but everything she saw was dim, distant, and obscured. The colors and clarity that I enjoyed as a matter of course were not available to her until she received some new aid to her vision from *outside of herself.*

This is us on a spiritual level—only we start off blind, not merely nearsighted. We need the Holy Spirit to open our eyes with the crystallized truth of the gospel. But he doesn't stop there. Over time, he sanctifies our vision by increasing our awareness of all that is lovely and true. Yet we are not mere passive recipients in this. Look at how the apostle Peter describes our part in the process:

> *For this very reason, make every effort to supplement*
> *your faith with virtue, and virtue with knowledge,*
> *and knowledge with self-control, and self-control with*
> *steadfastness, and steadfastness with godliness, and godliness*

*with brotherly affection, and brotherly affection with love.
For if these qualities are yours and are increasing, they keep
you from being ineffective or unfruitful in the knowledge of
our Lord Jesus Christ. For whoever lacks these qualities is so
nearsighted that he is blind, having forgotten that he was
cleansed from his former sins. Therefore, brothers, be all the
more diligent to confirm your calling and election, for if you
practice these qualities you will never fall. (2 Peter 1:5-10)*

Peter is saying, *Don't be nearsighted! The faith that was given
to you at the saving of your soul needs to be worked out in acts
of faith that will bear fruit in your life, if you don't slacken your
practice of them.*

We all want to be pastors who minister to our sheep with
the kinds of qualities listed in verses 5-7. Yet, according to
Peter, what leads to ineffectiveness and unfruitfulness is not,
at heart, a failure of diary management or a shortfall in funds.
It's forgetfulness: forgetting who we are, who God is, and
what he has done for us in cleansing us from our sin. When
we forget these things, we are self-deluded—the very opposite
of self-aware.

So what is it exactly that we need to remember?

What We Are Able to Do

Besides my work as a local church pastor, I have the privilege
of working with other church-planting pastors and their wives
in an organization called Harbor Network.

One of the things that makes us distinctive as a church-
planting network is our emphasis on helping pastors and their
wives to be whole and healthy people. To be honest, that's
actually our primary aim. It's one thing to plant a church; it's
another thing entirely to be a pastor who has the right things
implanted in you, so that your identity doesn't get caught up
in the maelstrom of day-to-day ministry life.

One of the most difficult things to reckon with, whether you're a first-year church-planter or a 50-year veteran of pastoral ministry, is that you will never have what it takes to take your ministry by storm—and praise God, because your people need a shepherd to lead them, not a rockstar to dazzle them.

As much as pastors need to guard their flock against ravenous wolves coming in to wreak havoc among them, they also need to guard their own hearts against ravenous, wolf-like desires that wear the sheep-like clothing of *good things*. You don't have to be around exhausted, on-the-edge-of-extinction pastors for too long before they tell you that the mile-long list of activities they're devoting themselves to are *all good things*. In his book *Counterfeit Gods*, Tim Keller writes, "Anything can serve as a counterfeit god, especially the very best things in life." The refusal to accept our limitations turns all the good things of our lives into "god things"—and that is very dangerous indeed.

One of the most difficult tasks for pastors of all ages and seasons is gaining a firm grasp on their limitations. It's true that if you put a group of pastors in a room together, they will likely all admit that, yes, they can't do it all, they can't be everything for everyone, and they certainly can't (aka shouldn't) cater to every whim and desire of their congregations. Admitting your limitations is part of what it looks like to be a humble pastor, after all. But living in light of those limitations is where wisdom comes in. Theorizing about our limitations does little good if we aren't daily grasping the reality that God didn't create us with hands big enough to hold *all things together*. There is only one person who can do that:

> *By [the Son] all things were created, in heaven and on earth, visible and invisible, whether thrones or dominions or rulers or authorities—all things were created through*

him and for him. And he is before all things, and in him all things hold together. And he is the head of the body, the church. He is the beginning, the firstborn from the dead, that in everything he might be preeminent.

(Colossians 1:16-18)

Look at the language the apostle Paul uses to describe Jesus: *by him, through him, in him, head of, the beginning, firstborn,* and *preeminent.* Last time I checked, I needed my iPhone to play a pretty little song every morning to even wake up on time. And that's just the beginning. I need a laundry list of baseline things (including, well, laundry) to even think about living a semi-normal, semi-adjusted life: food, water, clothing, shelter, and money. This doesn't even include all the spiritual and emotional needs I have that need to be met in order for me to be a somewhat whole and healthy person.

As Paul describes the absolute supremacy of Christ in Colossians 1, he reminds us of how different we are to this God. And yet it is this God who became one of us in order to save us: "Being found in human form, he humbled himself by becoming obedient to the point of death, even death on a cross" (Philippians 2:8). The key to godly self-awareness is to know how deeply dependent, inherently human, and fundamentally fragile you really are—*and* to trust that *Jesus knows* how true that is even more than you ever will. Take a moment to consider those two words: Jesus knows. This knowledge can leave us shuddering or soothed—but when we remember who Jesus is, the latter will be where our heart is most often moved.

The problem is that a dependent, fragile human is not the person I want to see when I look in the mirror on Monday morning. I want to see a strong, capable pastor who isn't subject to the same weaknesses as other mere mortals. I want phrases like "I don't know how you do it, Ronnie" and "God has gifted you in so many areas, brother" heaped upon me like gravy on Thanksgiving mashed potatoes. These are the perceptions I prefer people to have of me—because, as for Adam and Eve, the temptation to be like God is alluring.

Yet knowing *what we are able to do*—and, as we'll see later, *knowing what we are called to do*—is how we become pastors who are self-aware enough to do ministry at a sustainable pace. So let's take a look at a famous story in the Old Testament that will help us understand our limitations as leaders.

The Limitations of a Leader

The first place in Scripture where we see a practical example of leadership limitations comes from the story of Moses and Jethro in the book of Exodus. Moses' father-in-law, Jethro, pays a family visit to Moses and immediately observes a distinct lack of margin in Moses' life.

By this point in the narrative, the Israelites have come through the Red Sea and are now camping out in the desert. The chapter begins with Moses helping Jethro catch up on the story so far, and Jethro rejoicing "for all the good that the LORD had done" in delivering the Israelites "out of the hand of the Egyptians" (Exodus 18:9).

This is important to note: before Jethro even observed Moses' working methods, he saw the results of all that God was doing and recognized that it was praiseworthy work. As we talk about the limitations we have as leaders, we should also acknowledge the work that God has done and is doing through our limitations. Whether you feel like a leader with low, average, or high capacities, it's vital to remember that you do not limit God. Jethro's rejoicing testified to that truth, but so did his reaction to Moses after he got a more intimate look into his day-to-day routine. Check out this exchange between the two of them.

The next day Moses sat to judge the people, and the people stood around Moses from morning till evening. When Moses' father-in-law saw all that he was doing for the people, he said, "What is this that you are doing for the people? Why do you sit alone, and all the people stand around you from morning till evening?" And Moses said to his father-in-law, "Because the people come to me to inquire of God; when they have a dispute, they come to me and I decide between one person and another, and I make them know the statutes of God and his laws." Moses' father-in-law said to him, "What you are doing is not good. You and the people with you will certainly wear yourselves out, for the thing is too heavy for you. You are not able to do it alone."
(*Exodus 18:13-18*)

What Jethro observes is a glitch in Moses' leadership that has him doing far more than he is physically or mentally able to do, which we can wisely translate as *more than God had called him to do*. Pastors who insist on doing far more than they are physically and mentally able to do are ignoring the natural warning signs that God gives people to detect when they are operating outside of their limits. Thankfully, God often surrounds pastors with people like Jethro, who care enough about them to look closely at their lives and call them out. Do you have those people? And if so, do you actually listen to them?

Jethro wisely observes that Moses' role as Israel's arbiter over civil disputes is a subtle but significant shift from his original call, which was to be Israel's preacher:

Now obey my voice; I will give you advice, and God be with you! You shall represent the people before God and bring their cases to God, and you shall warn them about the statutes and the laws, and make them know the way in which they must walk and what they must do. (v 19-20)

Now that may be a fancy job description—but notice that people had let other tasks dominate Moses' duties instead.[16]

When a pastor becomes trapped in the minutiae of managing the church, their job description can easily morph into that of a supervisor or department head whose greatest tools become a bottle of aspirin in one hand and a fire extinguisher in the next.

Do pastors sometimes need extra-strength Tylenol or a trusty spiritual fire extinguisher at their disposal? That's a clear YES. But more importantly, they need to remember who they are when their hands are empty. They need to not forget that they are shepherds caring for God's sheep by the ordinary means of God's grace: through word and sacrament. Those are the required minimums that, unfortunately, we tend to minimize.

Jethro's honest assessment of Moses' workflow as being "not good" is related to the toll it would eventually take on Moses' health if he continued at this pace: "You and the people with you will certainly wear yourselves out, for the thing is too heavy for you. You are not able to do it alone" (v 18). Critique is never something we would describe as enjoyable, but Jethro's is incredibly gracious here, as he assures his son-in-law that God will be with him if he applies this good counsel (v 19) and returns to his primary call.[17]

Moses needed practical leadership counsel to see that living within his limitations would always include healthy delegation, since we are "not able to do it alone" (v 18b). Whether Jethro was addressing a portion of Moses' ego is not clear from the text. What is clear is that good leadership includes protection for personal health, which happens at a base level by establishing structures that hand appropriate responsibilities to other qualified men and women.[18]

In the end, "Moses listened to the voice of his father-in-law and did all that he said" (v 24). Recognizing his limitations, Moses followed Jethro's wise counsel and appointed a select but skilled number of people to share his leadership burden, thus contributing to his ongoing health as a leader. This wasn't just good for him, but for everyone: Moses' action plan drew more people into an active role in the covenant community, and meant that people got their cases resolved more efficiently (v 23). The fact that Moses' delegation process came through the wise counsel of another further illustrates that Moses was not only limited physically but mentally as well. As Proverbs reminds us, "A wise man listens to advice" (Proverbs 12:15b).

The story of Moses and Jethro reminds us that all pastoral skills are gifts from God that must be cultivated through the wise management of personal margin and limitations. Pastors who strive to accomplish every task that lies before them, while habitually ignoring their spiritual and physical needs, are in fact ignoring God's good intentions for human beings made in his image.

Solomon wrote that "it is in vain that you rise up early and go late to rest, eating the bread of anxious toil" (Psalm 127:2). When a pastor intentionally organizes his time in a way that testifies to the truth that "unless the LORD builds the house, those who build it labor in vain" (v 1), he will experience a ministry in which limitations are not merely tolerated but are received as occasions for deeper transformation, trust, and joy. Knowing *what we are able to do* is the only way we're going to actually live out *what we are called to do*.

What We Are Called to Do

Normally, this is the part of the chapter where I generate a list of things you can do to put its principles into practice. I want to be careful to not lay extra burdens on you that do nothing more than tempt you to try to exceed your limitations! But that said, let's get practical for a minute. How do I learn what my limitations actually are?

- Many of us who have been in ministry for some time usually acquire a decent grasp of what we're capable of and how we best operate. To use one example, some of us love to multitask—having a handful of projects, sermons, and ministry opportunities to work on is life-giving and invigorating. Others of us feel absolutely depleted when we have more than one project or task to accomplish at a time. It is not a defect if you find yourself squarely in this latter category. In fact, the fine art of delegation may come more naturally to you, whereas your multitasking counterpart might face significant struggles with that. The point is that we are all wired differently for a reason, so lean into that with grace and integrity.

- Like it or not, we are in an era when there is an abundance of personality tests to help us get a better grasp of who we are. Yes, we can place too much importance on things like Enneagram, Myers-Briggs, or StrengthsFinder. They certainly don't tell us everything we can know about our complex selves. But they can be helpful tools in clueing us in to some of the ways God has made us, which will then help us in determining our limitations as leaders.

- Finally, having a trusted friend or counselor is another way for us to better learn our limitations, as well as providing the encouragement and support we need to work through them.

With that said, let me end with a more reflective exercise by looking at three words that might offer us some help as we seek to grow in godly self-awareness regarding our limitations: *consider, call,* and *cast.*

Consider

> LORD, *our Lord,*
>   *how majestic is your name in all the earth!*
> *You have set your glory*
>   *in the heavens.*
> *Through the praise of children and infants*
>   *you have established a stronghold against your enemies,*
>   *to silence the foe and the avenger.*
> *When I consider your heavens,*
>   *the work of your fingers,*
> *the moon and the stars,*
>   *which you have set in place,*
> *what is mankind that you are mindful of them,*
>   *human beings that you care for them?*
>   *(Psalm 8:1-4, NIV)*

To become more aware of who God is, and who we are in light of that, requires us to be people who *consider*: who pause and reflect upon the grandeur of God and his creation. I love how David asks, "What is mankind?" In other words, *When I look up at the stars and behold the vast intricacies of the universe, I begin to understand how small I am and then begin to wonder why God has even taken notice of me at all.* You get this sense almost of dumbfoundedness from David.

When we give our minds the space to consider our benevolent Creator and his breathtaking creation, our self-awareness begins to grow by leaps and bounds, but without crushing us down into fine powder either. We remember that *though I may not be the biggest thing God has made, I am his most beloved.*

To consider these ginormous realities on a regular basis will inject a healthy level of sobriety into your soul. After all, God doesn't need your efforts to accomplish anything in this world, because he was able to speak it into existence. So you can be honest with yourself and others about what your limitations are, secure in your identity as one created by him. Those limitations don't make you "less than..." since God was *mindful* in how he created you. Remembering this will also stop you getting caught up in comparing yourself with others, because you know that God has created you to be uniquely you, and your limitations are part of his personal sovereign purposes.

Call

I love the LORD, because he has heard my voice
> *and my pleas for mercy.*
Because he inclined his ear to me,
> *therefore I will call on him as long as I live.*
The snares of death encompassed me;
> *the pangs of Sheol laid hold on me;*
> *I suffered distress and anguish.*
Then I called on the name of the LORD:
> *"O LORD, I pray, deliver my soul!"*

Gracious is the LORD, and righteous;
> *our God is merciful.*
The LORD preserves the simple;
> *when I was brought low, he saved me.*
Return, O my soul, to your rest;
> *for the LORD has dealt bountifully with you.*
> > *(Psalm 116:1-7)*

Healthy self-awareness brings us to a place of sweet but also desperate vulnerability before the Lord. The song above contains the words of a man who knows himself and where he needs to go for help. It's not polite, nor is it sanitized. These are raw, unfiltered pleas from the depths of one man's soul straight to the divine ears of the Lord. The psalmist has a good grasp on reality—and notice that it doesn't lead him into greater self-sufficiency but into total dependency on the Lord. He calls on the name of the Lord in his distress and anguish, reminding himself that the Lord is gracious and merciful, and saves those who are experiencing the lowest of lows. This is the model for how a self-aware believer finds rest for their soul from the Savior of their soul. Admittedly, I read this and think, "Golly, what a horrible place to be in." And yet, this is the place I will find rest in if I make the right *call*.

This is bewildering to me in some ways. The "calls" I make when I'm in distress are usually ones that keep me frantic and harried because they're quick, aspirin-like fixes to help alleviate my pain but only temporarily. For me, it might be buying something I don't need on Amazon Prime, indulging in something sweet and sugary, or scrolling mindlessly through YouTube or Twitter/X. These may seem like fairly harmless forms of self-medication in the grand scheme of things, but the bigger point is that if I'm not making a beeline to the throne of grace, I'm only dulling and diluting my pain rather than seeking divine comfort. It means that I'm not able to instruct and direct my soul to its rest because I've failed to seek the Lord's bountiful provision.

Make the right call.

Cast

> *Humble yourselves, therefore, under the mighty hand of God so that at the proper time he may exalt you, casting all your anxieties on him, because he cares for you.*
> *(1 Peter 5:6-7)*

Look, I am no fisherman. In fact, my brother and I still joke about the fact that in all the times our dad took us fishing when we were growing up, we never caught one fish. You didn't read that wrong. Not one, my friend.

Peter points out that we will have a much better success rate when we cast our anxieties on the Lord and reel in his fatherly and compassionate care as the result. Of course, he prefaces this idea of casting our anxieties there by saying that it's going to require humility. Casting our anxieties on the Lord happens when we acknowledge that we cannot keep our world spinning. As a pastor, I find things are constantly slipping out of my grasp. The question is not whether things are slipping (because they are), but how I respond to all the things that my two medium-sized hands cannot contain no matter how hard I try and hold on.

It's like a kid putting a quarter into the candy machine to get a handful of Skittles or M&Ms. The minute they turn the handle, their hands are never able to hold all the candy that comes pouring out, so they frantically try everything they can to stop it from running all over the ground. For many of us, this is a metaphor for our ministries, if we're being honest: everything spilling all over and us frantically trying to stop the mess. Except, we can't. As Zack Eswine wisely writes in his book *The Imperfect Pastor*, "You and I were never meant to repent for not being everywhere for everybody and all at once. You and I are meant to repent because we've tried to be."

How do I end this? Certainly not by chastising you into just "being more self-aware." Instead, let me invite you to become more aware of your Savior first.

The good news is: *you don't got this.*

But he does.

Now to him who is able to do far more abundantly than all that we ask or think, according to the power at work within us, to him be glory in the church and in Christ Jesus throughout all generations, forever and ever. Amen.
(Ephesians 3:20-21)

CHAPTER FIVE

Contemplation

"I don't want to have to think about it."

As I've gotten older, this phrase seems to come out of my mouth more and more often. Pastoring can require a lot of my physical energy, but it probably takes more of my mental energy than anything else. Even as I'm writing this chapter, I still have a sermon to write for Sunday, a talk to complete for an upcoming pastors and wives' retreat, two magazine articles due in ten days, and Sunday-school materials to prepare for, well, Sunday. Have I mentioned elders' meetings, lunch appointments, video recordings, and zoom calls? Have I mentioned that I have a wife who wouldn't mind seeing me on occasion too? This succession of seemingly unending tasks can feel relentless when I type them out like this. If they caused you anxiety by just reading them, I'm really sorry.

One of the problems that our crowded task-lists present is a loss of margin and space. When we find ourselves going from one thing to another without a minute to stop and breathe, we can begin to operate like machines—which would be fantastic if God had designed us as machines. But he didn't. God created us as human beings, who lack, intentionally, the mechanized ability to continue working *ad infinitum*, without rest or reflection.

What's problematic is that many of us kind of *like* moving through life in a machine-like manner. We like going from one task to another, getting stuff done, making decisions, and crossing off all the tasks on our ministry to-do lists. There is something invigorating and empowering about that. A sense of invincibility can sweep over us, and we can begin to tell ourselves, "You got this!"

Which would be great, if it wasn't for this one "glitch" in our human operating system: we don't "got" this. That's the lie that stretches all the way back to Genesis 3. Behind the words "Did God really say?" spoken to Adam and Eve was the insinuation that they didn't need the good plan that God had purposed for them before the foundation of the world. *You don't need God. You got this.* (Quick qualifier here—don't hear me saying you're speaking the words of Satan if you use this phrase. Telling your friend "You got this" before they jump into a difficult task, sporting event, financial decision, and so on, can be a great encouragement. Anyway, I think you know what I mean. You got this.)

In regards to ministry, a "you got this" mentality will exhibit itself as a pastor who doesn't see a contemplative character as an internal muscle worth developing. What Adam and Eve did when they were tempted by Satan was what many of us do when faced with a big decision, which is, we jump in immediately. We give ourselves no time to think, seek good counsel, pray, or consider the short- and long-term consequences. Imagine how different things may have been if Eve had been a bit more thoughtful, curious, and contemplative after her dialogue with the serpent. Imagine if she and Adam had discussed the serpent's offer among themselves and then taken their concerns to the Lord as they strolled together in the cool of the garden? How different would things be right now? (I probably wouldn't be writing a book on unhurriedness for pastors, I'll tell you that much.)

Instead, Adam and Eve didn't want to have to think about it, and then made the gravest mistake in all of human history.

Literally.

What Do We Mean When We Say Contemplative?

A contemplative person is someone who gives prolonged thought to any given matter, decision, concept, conflict, or situation. In other words, "a very thoughtful person."

When we use the word "contemplative," we're not talking about someone who spends too much time *overthinking* everything. This is a person who develops unhealthy habits of procrastination, laboring too long on simple tasks or falling into paralysis when it comes to making decisions, however large or small. For the overthinker, developing a more truly contemplative spirit (by the power of the Spirit) will help them push through their fear of failure and letting people down, and the tendency to feel that they're being judged with every word they utter and stroke of the keyboard. Contemplation provides the space for us to differentiate between what is true and what is not so that we develop healthier patterns of working and thinking.

When I think of thoughtful people in my life, my mind immediately goes to two of the original elders of our church. Jeff and Dave were in their late 50s and early 70s respectively when they became part of our eldership team (and Jeff is still on the team). Jeff was a former lead pastor and later a district superintendent in the Evangelical Free Church of America for 18 years. Dave was also a former lead pastor, who transitioned into overseas mission work, primarily in Romania, where he helped start a seminary to train local pastors and church planters. When they joined our church's eldership, they had about 60 years of ministry experience between them, so you can imagine how thrilled I was to have their collective wisdom help me lead our new church as a young whippersnapper in my early 40s. It was the Lord's gracious and providential hand on my life to have two men of this caliber alongside me so early on.

In the rest of this chapter, I want to share some of the ways in which Jeff and Dave brought the rare and beautiful quality of contemplation to their role as elders. My hope is that by sharing some personal stories from the trenches of local ministry, we might gain a greater understanding of why becoming more contemplative should be a chief aspiration for our life.

They were not in a hurry

Let's be honest. Ministry means that sometimes we are faced with decisions that have to be made quickly. When things break down on a physical, emotional, or relational level, we are forced to make quick decisions for the safety and well-being of everyone involved. When a pipe breaks in the church bathroom and the water begins to gush out like a mini-Niagara Falls, we don't have time to sit back and contemplate the best ways to address the situation. What we need is a plumber to come out as soon as possible and stop the broken pipe from doing further damage. When we find out someone in the church is caught in an abusive situation, we need to act as swiftly as possible in order to protect them from further danger. Those are just two examples where acting quickly and decisively is the wisest and most loving approach we can take.

With that said, most of the situations we find ourselves in (even conflict situations) are not *crisis* situations. We usually have some *time*. Time to not be in a hurry, time to discuss different ideas and options, and time to give those ideas and options space to marinate in our hearts and minds. The way of wisdom is not treating every decision as a crisis that needs to be handled as quickly and urgently as possible.

I remember one particular occasion early on in our church plant when I thought everything was moving too slowly: church growth, finding a better gathering space, discipling our people, and starting membership classes. The response from both Jeff and Dave was to sit back and recount all the amazing things God had already done in such a short amount of time. What they were trying to do (very kindly and gently) was to create a culture of awareness for all God was doing. Those other things would come *tomorrow*, but they didn't want me to miss what God was doing *today*.

That was by no means the only such occasion. When I think back years later, I remain stunned by the patience that Jeff and Dave brought into our meetings when I would bring matters to the table that needed to be discussed and decided. To be honest, I would sometimes interpret their lack of hurriedness as an absence of care or understanding, but it turns out that I was usually the one who was lacking both of those things. When we remove hurry from our decision-making process, we are actually leaning *more* deeply into care and understanding. We are allowing wisdom to be what guides us rather than our initial thoughts or emotions.

> *Desire without knowledge is not good,*
> *and whoever makes haste with his feet misses his way.*
> *(Proverbs 19:2)*

As pastors, we need to *lean* as much as we *lead*, and probably more. What I mean is that when you are leaning against a wall, for example, you have stopped walking. You are able to observe what's around you, listen more intently if someone needs your ear, plot where you're going next with greater perspective, and then step in the right direction and take others with you. If I'm *leaning* into the ways of Jesus by resisting a hurried life, I'm going to be a pastor who is *leading* with a much less harried heart. Jeff and Dave had developed a seasoned pattern of not making haste with their feet, and every time I slowed my feet down to listen to them, I gained a renewed level of knowledge that helped reorder my desires.

They prayed about everything

Does this seem obvious? It shouldn't, and I only say that because you can probably all compile a list from here to the planet Mars of the decisions you've made (personally and pastorally) that have been completely devoid of prayer. When hurriedness is our default setting, prayer is the one thing we don't seem to get to. The best decision we can land on before making a decision is prayer. I will cover the topic of prayer in another chapter at greater length, but for now, remember that prayer is a tangible way of admitting to the Lord, ourselves, and to one another that "we don't got this." It's hitting pause before hitting play. It's giving your head, heart, and hands unhurried time to *lean* into where the Lord is leading you before you *lead* people in the way of the Lord.

With Jeff and Dave, we would pray about *everything*. Nothing was too small or too insignificant, and that's because nothing *is* too small or insignificant. Now, don't take this too far, because certain items (on, say, an elders' meeting agenda) require greater attention than others, and we need to use good discernment to ensure that we are stewarding our time well. What Jeff and Dave taught me as a hurried pastor in a fierce battle with his humanity was that prayer is the first recourse of wise people.

> Do not be anxious about anything, but in everything by prayer and supplication with thanksgiving let your requests be made known to God. (Philippians 4:6)

Here's what usually happened after we spent time praying during one of our elders' meetings. Over the next day or so, I would get a text, email, or phone call from Jeff or Dave to discuss one or more of the items we prayed about. Often we landed on a particular decision, but all of us came back a day or two later with a wiser and more thoughtful perspective. I remember one time in particular: it was about how we were going to approach a certain church member with a sin issue, and we all came to the conclusion that there was a better way to approach them than we originally had discussed!

Prayer opened our hearts to deeper spiritual insights, more prudent practical implications, and more creative ideas to share with one another. Why is that? Because prayer creates perspective. And boy, do we ever need more of that!

They were curious about what God was doing

The contemplative pastor is one who is armed with a spiritual telescope and a spiritual microscope at all times. By this I mean that we develop a godly curiosity about what God is doing both up close and far away. I mean, we know that God's will is our sanctification (1 Thessalonians 4:3), but we need to be curious about the variety of ways in which he is sanctifying us, and our members, so that we can better shepherd our people.

The pandemic will no doubt be one of the church's historical touchpoints for years to come. At the heart of countless conversations among pastors during COVID was the question, "What do you think God is doing?" (By the way, if it takes a pandemic for us to begin seriously asking that question, we need to ask what the cause might be for our profound lack of curiosity.)

> *If people can't see what God is doing, they stumble all over themselves; But when they attend to what he reveals, they are most blessed (Proverbs 29:18, MSG).*

In my years with Jeff and Dave, I noticed a godly curiosity in them to see what God was doing and how God was moving, and how we could better become part of that work.

I remember one instance when we were having a slight disagreement on some ideas I had for how to develop our children's ministry. I asked them to stretch their thinking and our philosophy in this area, because I saw an opportunity with the growth we were experiencing to expand our vision. At some point I felt they were being overly cautious, but later I realized they were likely being more curious about what God was doing so that we respond most appropriately. They didn't want to move so fast that we stumbled all over ourselves; instead they wanted to attend to what God was making plain to us at that moment. They took out their spiritual microscopes and looked at some of the granular ways in which God was blessing our growing church. They also took out their telescopes and adjusted the lens to see how God might be moving as we peeked into the future. It takes a contemplative (and courageous) heart to stop long enough to lean in and be curious about the ways in which the Lord is leading.

You might not always like what you see.

But you will see.

They were hopeful for the future

I don't think this is exclusively a generational thing, but my generation (Gen-X) can tend to be—how can I say this nicely—somewhat *cynical* when it comes to the future. I, by no means, buck that trend. Whether it's due to nature or nurture (though it's probably due to both), I'm not always the most optimistic person when it comes to the future. Yet developing a more contemplative spirit will help me, and other pastors like me, become more hopeful. Why is that? Because when we pause long enough to give our thoughts over to the greatness of God, the love of Jesus, and the work of the Holy Spirit, our souls cynicism will be swallowed up in hopefulness.

That may sound overly simple or naive, but hopefulness certainly wasn't simple or naive for Jeff and Dave. You can only imagine the difficult things these two brothers have seen when you total all their ministry years. Yet they remain hopeful for the future. They have known plenty of wreckage and ruin, but they don't let those experiences make them distrustful of God, suspicious of his grace, or resentful toward his people.

What I learned from these brothers is that they always thought the best of others. One time in particular, Dave and I sat down with a disgruntled couple who accused me of—I'm not joking here—*preaching the gospel too much*. They claimed that I was missing the opportunity to delve deeper into things like history and tradition in my sermons, for example. They may have been right, too, because those are not areas I spend a lot of time on. Nevertheless, it was a difficult meeting since they were very passionate in their communication. The thing that sticks out to me the most, though, was how patient Dave was. He never lost his temper, raised his voice, or lost faith that God was working in this young couple's life. He thanked them for the time they had given to being part of our congregation and remained friends with them even after they departed.

How could this be? The answer is that Dave practiced the contemplative art of gratefulness. He didn't reduce everything in life to pluses and minuses but received everything that happened in his life as a movement of God's gracious hand.

I will give thanks to the LORD with my whole heart;
I will recount all of your wonderful deeds. (Psalm 9:1)

King David was a man who had lived on the edge of his own extinction for years. He had had so many reasons to have grown hopeless given the relentless number of downturns his life had taken. As pastors, we may not be fighting giants, facing off against enemy nations, or fleeing for our life from our children, but we do find ourselves in our own hopeless deserts just like David—and just like David, we would do well to recount the wonderful deeds of the Lord as we thank him with our whole hearts. It's not that we have nothing to be thankful for; it's that the things we are not very thankful for can come in at the loudest volume.

Allow me to sound slightly cranky for a second: one thing that I intensely dislike is live music in a restaurant. I'm not anti live music—I'm a musician, for crying out loud. It's just that when I meet a friend at a restaurant, my desire is to have a fun, engaging, and peaceable conversation. When live music is playing, it's usually all you can hear, and your conversations will suffer as a result.

What you're probably taking away from this is that I'm not a super-fun dude. But my real point is that all kinds of things can threaten to be the loudest voice in your head and heart, but you need to turn down those volumes so that hopefulness becomes the louder voice. David did it through recounting God's wondrous deeds. Jeff and Dave did it in the same way. To be a person who recounts the wondrous deeds of the Lord requires time for prolonged thoughts and prayers, and to give your heart the margin it needs to be reshaped through the act of being grateful to God.

They had a settled joy

This is a big one. If you ever get the chance to meet Jeff and Dave, you will witness what I call a *settled joy* in them. This particular type of joy most commonly comes through experiencing the refining fire of the Lord. In fact, you could argue that it can't come in any other way. Becoming a contemplative person—who *leans* on the Lord before *leading* the Lord's people—means your spirit will have time to become content in the secure love of Jesus. The apostle Paul talked about this settled sense of joy when he said, "I have learned in whatever situation I am to be content. I know how to be brought low, and I know how to abound. In any and every circumstance, I have learned the secret of facing plenty and hunger, abundance and need" (Philippians 4:11-12).

When I think about Jeff and Dave, I think about two men who have learned the *secret*. Except it's not really a secret. It's simply a matter of knowing the settled face and steady hand of Jesus in every unsettled situation, looking to him to calm all of your internal turmoil. I wish I was describing something easy, but you all know that I'm not. We know that "godliness with contentment is great gain" (1 Timothy 6:6), but the steps to gaining that contentment can feel bewildering.

Ultimately, settled joy comes through a constant refilling of all that is good. It comes by embracing a more contemplative life that will *lead* you to *lean* into prioritizing unhurriedness, prayer, curiosity, and hopefulness—practices that will produce a more settled, unhurried joy as you begin to see slowness as next to godliness.

But you'll have to stop and lean against the wall in order to imagine what might happen.

> *I have set the LORD always before me;*
>   *because he is at my right hand, I shall not be shaken.*
> *Therefore my heart is glad, and my whole being rejoices;*
>   *my flesh also dwells secure. (Psalm 16:8-9)*

CHAPTER SIX

Prayer

Well, this one should seem obvious, huh?

I wish it was.

I was at a pastors' conference years ago and heard one of the main speakers say, "Brothers, we are all terrible at prayer." I remember thinking, "I didn't think pastors had the option of being terrible at prayer."

Of all the things a pastor has to do, and there are many, a pastor's job is to *pray*. Does that hit you funny? What if I framed it like this—*you are paid to pray*. That probably hit you even funnier. This is not the kind of motivational phrase that should make it onto the front of your coffee mug, but I think it's vital to see prayer not as something you do when you get around to it but as something that is part and parcel of who you are as a *person* who *pastors* God's people in the humility of your humanity.

The German Reformer Martin Luther is supposed to have famously said something to the effect of "I have so much to do that I shall spend the first three hours in prayer." One thing which that points to is the *peculiar productivity of prayer*.

I like using the word *productivity* because it's a word we understand and really like, if we're being honest. We tend to think of "productive" activity as *something we do that produces a result we can see.* This is difficult for pastors, though, because other than our sermon, we don't typically have a "product" for people to see which allows them to easily measure what we've been doing all week. This is because pastoral ministry is generally busier with the productivity of the *heart* than with the productivity of the *hands*. Although that's right and true, this lack of any measurable product can create all kinds of internal angst. Why is that? I believe it's because we like measurable things, and we're pretty sure our congregations like them too. So when we hear another joke about pastors only "working one day a week," we may have to laugh it off in order to be good sports, but it compounds our fears around how people perceive our work.

Pastors, we need to get back to prayer. Why? Well, for a whole load of reasons. But for the purpose of this book, we'll focus on one: because prayer forms our hearts, and un-hurries our hands in the process.

A Good Habit

Curiously, I find that whenever we get to the word "formation," we seem to run into something that feels less tangible, less "meat on the bones", and far too ethereal for our tastes. It might be helpful to remember that although prayer *forms* us, it doesn't *fix* us. It is a habit that is meant to change us. But that takes time.

It's a little like how my wife waters her garden. She will stand out in the fiery heat for what seems like hours, making sure everything is watered properly. Thankfully, the minute after she finishes her watering, all of these beautiful, ginormous vegetables just fall off the vines, and we pile them up in our baskets to bring into the kitchen…

Obviously, that is *not* how it works.

The watering process is slow and painful, and after she's done, all you can see is a wet and muddy garden, with some of her plants buried underneath what looks like a small pond of water. If you didn't know what was coming, you'd wonder why on earth she insists on getting these plants so wet all the time. Eventually, though, there's something lovely that comes through my wife's persistent watering, and it's all these beautiful varieties of vegetables in all kinds of vibrant shapes and colors.

Prayer works like that. It's like water in the garden of our soul. It's doing something beneath the surface of our being that we can't always see but that we trust is going to produce something lovely—as long as we don't break our habit of consistent watering.

Said like this, prayer seems like a breeze, doesn't it? The problem is that we want to work to shorter time scales. So when it comes to prayer, we don't often believe it is working.

It's this reason (and many more, I'm sure) that results in lackluster prayer lives in pastors—and that leaves us working harder and harder to compensate for everything we don't believe prayer is actually accomplishing.

Few of us would ever care to admit this though, would we? We are supposed to be the bonafide "prayer warriors" of our churches.

Could this wording be part of our problem? I'm going to take a leap here and say that we should instead aim to become "prayer mail carriers."

Go with me here.

My sister was a mail carrier for a few years, and every day you would find her walking through the same neighborhood, delivering mail into the same mailboxes and waving hello to the same neighbors. Although she delivered her mail in a timely and efficient manner on Monday, she still needed to do it again on Tuesday. She could not deliver all the mail for the week in one day. It required faithful, consistent, day-in-and-day-out work. A warrior, on the other hand, is someone who slays dragons—and dragon-slaying is frantic and intense work that comes in fits and spurts.

By the way, it's fine if you like using "prayer warrior" language—I'm just trying to make the point that forming more consistent habits of prayer will be what contributes to a less hurried way of being. And those habits look like anything that is habitual in our lives. For example, there are things that have become so ingrained in my day that I have to intentionally *not do them* in order to divert from the norm: eating, showering, brushing my teeth, putting on my shoes, or checking my phone are just a few of the many habitual things that happen like clockwork. Our hope should be that prayer becomes this habitual for us, so that if a day goes by in the absence of prayer, it would be a rare and unusual occurrence of events.

For the record, this chapter is not meant to be a crash course in prayer. There are so many good books devoted entirely to the topic, and you've likely read more than a few of them. At the end of the chapter, I want to take a more in-depth look at why we don't believe prayer works. Before that, I thought it might be helpful to answer a few baseline questions related to prayer so that we are reminded that, without the habit of it, we have no hope of becoming unhurried pastors.

Why Should I Pray?

Prayer is how I experience the peace of God, protect my heart from anxiety, and reposition it to rejoice

> *Rejoice in the Lord always; again I will say, rejoice. Let your reasonableness be known to everyone. The Lord is at hand; do not be anxious about anything, but in everything by prayer and supplication with thanksgiving let your requests be made known to God. And the peace of God, which surpasses all understanding, will guard your hearts and your minds in Christ Jesus. (Philippians 4:4-7)*

How on earth do we get our hearts to the place that Paul is urging—no, *commanding*—us to get to: a place of rejoicing and peace? Paul tells us in the middle of these verses: we pray. "In everything by prayer and supplication with thanksgiving let your requests be made known to God" (v 6).

Prayer is how I have God's ear

We know that God does not listen to sinners, but if anyone is a worshiper of God and does his will, God listens to him.
(John 9:31)

Remember the story of the blind man whom Jesus heals by anointing his eyes with mud? Unsurprisingly, the Pharisees, because they refuse to believe it was Jesus who healed the man, begin to harass the man and his parents. One of my favorite parts of the story is in this verse, when the man starts preaching to the Pharisees, reminding them that God listens to all those who worship him and do his will. The Pharisees are less than happy, but we learn something important about prayer in this exchange: God's people have God's ear.

Imagine being able to express your every thought, disappointment, sin, hope, fear, failure, evil thought, angry impulse, and happiness, and every dream you've never talked about to anyone else in the world. Then imagine the smile that comes over God's face, the understanding in his eyes, and the love in his voice as he listens to your every word.

You have your Father's ear. All you have to do is speak to him.

Prayer is how I confess my sins and become conformed to God's will

Draw near to God, and he will draw near to you. Cleanse your hands, you sinners, and purify your hearts, you double-minded. (James 4:8)

Sin is always crouching at the door, seeking to master us as it did Adam and Eve's son Cain (Genesis 4:7). Some sins stick to us too. They've formed habits and patterns that are incredibly difficult for us to break. What Jesus does is *transform* us by reordering our desires toward pursuing holiness.

When did you last pray that God would guard you against a nagging sin or harmful habit that you've formed? It may be that you've not progressed much in your battle with certain sins because you haven't developed a habit of prayer to combat what's really going on: a spiritual battle. I want to be careful, because it could be that you've prayed diligently for years over besetting sins and still struggle greatly with them. There is grace and good hope for you, even in the mire of shame and discouragement that these kinds of relentless sins and temptations can bring. Prayer is how we equip ourselves for battle; and prayer is how we find healing for our wounds: "If we confess our sins, he is faithful and just to forgive us our sins and to cleanse us from all unrighteousness" (1 John 1:9).

What Should I Pray?

When it comes to the content of our prayer, Jesus gave us a model.

> *And he said to them, "When you pray, say:*
> *"Father, hallowed be your name.*
> *Your kingdom come.*
> *Give us each day our daily bread,*
> *and forgive us our sins, for we ourselves forgive everyone*
> *   who is indebted to us.*
> *And lead us not into temptation." (Luke 11:2-4)*

1. *Hallowed:* Sometimes, when I was a kid, my dad would say something like "Remember who you're talking to" when my mouth got a little saucy. This isn't quite the same thing, but when we pray in the way Jesus

instructed his disciples to, we begin by remembering who we are talking to: the almighty God of the universe, whose name is worthy of reverence and awe. Beginning our prayers by acknowledging the hallowed name of God also reminds us that he is over all the things that we feel we need to be over but actually can't be. When we are faced with a ministry crisis like suffering, anxiety, or stress, remembering the hallowedness of God will help us with the hurriedness that threatens our hearts.

2. *Kingdom come:* When we are running on our own steam, we are likely not walking in line with the things that God prioritizes for his people. Praying, "Your kingdom come" is how we realign our will with God's will, and remember to love what he loves and hate what he hates. We live as people who are becoming more kingdom-minded in our thinking, loving, and living. This frame of mind and posture of heart give us perspective as we pray. When we are tempted to rush around building our own mini-kingdoms within the walls of our church, praying "your kingdom come" reorients us to something bigger.

3. *Daily bread:* We should never forget to pray for our basic necessities, like food, water, and clothing. When we ask the Lord to give us our daily bread, we are seeking God to be the Giver of all good things, and taking care to remember that he joyfully supplies all our needs. If the goodness of the Lord is so great that he cares about the most basic of our needs, what does this tell us about the other needs that tend to leave us frantic and forlorn in ministry? That's right: he cares about those too. By praying for our daily bread, we remember God's heart for the details in our life that we have a tendency to dismiss.

4. *Forgive us our sins:* Seeing ourselves in the way Paul saw himself, as the chief of all sinners (1 Timothy 1:15), is how we will stop operating at a pace that fools us and others into thinking that we are like God. We need our souls cleansed and our spirits renewed because we are, as one old hymn puts it, "prone to wander."[19] And wandering is how we lose the plot of God's kingdom narrative for our lives—a narrative that finds us not only seeking God's forgiveness but able to shower others with the abundance of what we have received. Regular times of confession keep our heart cleansed before the Lord and allow us to minister without guilty consciences hampering our soul.

5. *Lead us not into temptation:* When we talk about a hurried pastor, we are talking about a person who has given in to the temptation to pastor in a way that denies his humanity. Gaining the strength and humility to guard against this kind of temptation will only come through the habit of prayer. Wonderfully, the Lord is eager to guard us against this temptation. He tells us to ask for the moral and physical strength we need precisely so that he can give it.

When Should I Pray?

Pray always

Rejoice always, pray without ceasing, give thanks in all circumstances; for this is the will of God in Christ Jesus for you. (1 Thessalonians 5:16-18)

This Martin Lloyd-Jones quote is so good that I just had to mention it: "Always respond to every impulse to pray."[20] I get it: "praying without ceasing" can sound like something that's impossible to carry out, but I think another way to phrase it might be *having an ongoing conversation with God.*

I like to use the example of texting my wife. Since we are not physically in each other's presence every waking hour of every day, texting has been a way for us to have an ongoing conversation wherever we are. It's so helpful to know what the other person is up to, what kind of day they're having, how we can pray for one another, and a million other things that keep us close and informed even though we may be miles apart.

In a similar way, having an ongoing conversation with God keeps us close to him, mindful of his presence, and aware that he is on the move no matter what kind of day we're having.

Pray when you're with others

All these with one accord were devoting themselves to prayer, together with the women and Mary the mother of Jesus, and his brothers. (Acts 1:14)

Therefore, confess your sins to one another and pray for one another, that you may be healed. The prayer of a righteous person has great power as it is working. (James 5:16)

Praying with others is one of the ways in which we lower our guard and show our humanity. There is something in the public act of praying that is very humbling. We are pausing in order to plead for the Lord's help. Many times when we're with either a group or a person, we can circle around an issue or problem and then leave without once laying it before the Lord. In a sense, we never get the kind of "closure" that prayer provides. Again, our issues or problems won't typically get fixed through one prayer, but one prayer is another opportunity to acknowledge before God and others that we certainly can't fix anything without him.

Why Pastors Fail to Pray

If you've ever thumbed through a copy of *Us Weekly* magazine while waiting for an appointment at the doctor's office or getting an oil change in your car, you may have come to a section called, "Stars–They're Just Like Us!" This is where you catch a rare glimpse of Hollywood celebs doing all the same things that—gasp!—normal people do, such as ordering a coffee at Starbucks, picking up their dry cleaning, tying their kids' shoes, or grabbing a Quarter Pounder at McDonald's.

When it comes to pastors and prayer, we are just like the people we pastor, who struggle to pray as they ought. Keep in mind that what follows is not meant to condemn you if you have a lackluster prayer life. The aim is renew your belief in the grace that God provides through prayer, so that you don't "lose heart" (Luke 18:1).

So why do pastors fail to pray?

We don't feel the immediate effects of prayer

This is a universal struggle for all pastors and all Christians. Sometimes prayer feels like speaking words into the wind. Most of us know on an intellectual level that prayer changes things, but because those changes aren't instantaneous, we can choose shortcuts and take matters into our own hands. By nature, prayer is about waiting: waiting on the Lord to act at a time that only he knows best. Because of this, prayer can leave us feeling a bit emotionally cold at times.

But I think this comes from the fundamental misunderstanding that prayer is supposed to always provide me with a feeling, sensation, or outcome that is tangibly felt right away. In this sense, prayer becomes a sort of spiritual ibuprofen. It's meant to alleviate my pain immediately and put a swing back in my step so that I can reenter the fray without any nagging discomfort. The problem is that prayer doesn't always work like that. It is less like a painkiller that we pop in our mouths and more like our required daily water consumption. We are encouraged to drink a lot of water so that our bodies are properly hydrated and we experience greater health benefits as a result. Now, what I *immediately* experience when I'm well hydrated are many, many trips to the restroom (sorry for this graphic imagery, friends). But eventually, if I keep it up, I benefit from improved brain performance, greater energy during the day, a healthier heart, better functioning organs… and if I keep going this is going to turn into a medical journal. Being well hydrated just keeps my body functioning in the way it is supposed to function.

When we don't keep ourselves spiritually well hydrated through constant prayer, our hearts aren't going to function in the way they're supposed to function: with hope. Instead, we will be seeking that hope through a variety of painkiller-like activities that may give us temporary relief but are not really addressing the deeper dilemmas that only prayer has the power to resolve.

Remember the analogy that James gives us regarding farmers:

> *Be patient, therefore, brothers, until the coming of the Lord. See how the farmer waits for the precious fruit of the earth, being patient about it, until it receives the early and the late rains. You also, be patient. Establish your hearts, for the coming of the Lord is at hand. (James 5:7-8)*

A farmer doesn't dig up his seeds the day after he plants them to see if there's been any growth. That would destroy his crop. Instead, the farmer waits with patience for the early and late rains because he believes that the fruit that will be produced one day will be precious. Praying is like planting seeds in some ways. We deposit our hopes, dreams, groanings, and complaints into the soil of God's heart, and we wait for the early and late rains that he provides to us in his own good timing. The result is that we grow in patience and hope for the precious fruit that we trust will come at harvest time. You don't just pray to receive something immediately (though God grants our immediate requests at times) but to gain a heart that is anchored by the weight of hope of what will one day come in glory.

We don't believe we will receive the answer we want

The second reason why pastors often fail to pray is that we don't believe we'll receive the answer we want. This reminds me of when I was a kid and wanted something big and expensive from my parents, like a pair of shoes, a bicycle, or a backpack. Before asking them for it, I would try and determine if it was something I could somehow buy for myself because there was nothing worse than getting the dreaded "no" from them. I think we do this with the Lord sometimes; we arbitrarily determine that he doesn't want to give us the good gift we request, so we take matters into our own hands.

We've probably experienced this in other facets of life. Imagine being in a job where you are not given the tools to accomplish your tasks, or in a relationship where you ask a friend or spouse for better communication so that you can contribute to the relationship in more helpful ways, only for none of those things to be forthcoming. Both of these circumstances would result in frustration and despondency because, no matter how much we ask, we never get what we need.

Thankfully, our requests don't work like this when it comes to the Lord. The late Tim Keller stated it well when he said, "God will either give us what we ask or give us what we would have asked if we knew everything he knows."[21] This statement just knocks me off my feet. You mean I don't always know what's best for me? You mean when God answers my prayers with "no" or "wait," he is actually giving me the best answer I could possibly have? Yes and yes!

See, when I withhold my prayers from God because I don't believe he will provide me with the answer I want, my only alternative is to take matters into my own hands and provide myself with what I want as quickly as I can. It's in this moment that I'm distrusting the goodness of God and his intentions toward me.

My point is that God is never withholding something good from you—and even when it is a genuinely *good* thing that we've asked for and not received, we can trust that it would only produce a bad thing in us if granted, or prevent a better thing that we will gain in waiting for it or in the lack of it altogether. The psalmist gives us a gentle reminder here:

> For the LORD God is a sun and shield;
>   the LORD bestows favor and honor.
> No good thing does he withhold
>   from those who walk uprightly. (Psalm 84:11)

It's hard for me to fathom this statement: "no good thing." I guess I need to go back to the whiteboard once again and rewrite my definitions of what I consider to be *good*. It turns out that they could use some editing. For example:

- God has a good reason why that tension with a particular church member has not been resolved. What do I need to learn about myself? How might I grow in greater grace?

- God has a good purpose for not growing my church as quickly as I hoped. What is he teaching me about my metric for success? What are some things he is allowing me to see that growth might blind me to?

I don't want to oversimplify this, though—we can and will experience significant pain when it comes to how God answers our prayers.

Maybe you were expecting that sentence to end, "when it comes to *unanswered prayers*." But our prayers never go *unanswered*. We get a *yes*, a *no*, or a *wait*, and all three are answers. Answers without defects, by the way:

Every good gift and every perfect gift is from above, coming down from the Father of lights, with whom there is no variation or shadow due to change. (James 1:17)

Sometimes, this can feel rough. A *no* or a *wait* can keep us in dimly lit places of pain or unsettled in days of suspended animation. If only we had a Father who was so good that we could trust him not only to give us what we need but even things we want on occasion!

I'm telling you, we do. If you don't believe me, Jesus is very clear:

If you then, who are evil, know how to give good gifts to your children, how much more will the heavenly Father give the Holy Spirit to those who ask him! (Luke 11:13)

Since he's a good Father, God uses our prayers to give us good things and also to change things for our good. Not because our words are magic but because God responds to the heart behind them and changes our heart through his answers to them. Pastor John Piper said:

Draw near in prayer to the throne of grace, bow down before its majestic authority, and on your knees drink from the river of the water of life that flows from the throne of God.[22]

This is the great power that comes through the habit of prayer. It renews us, it forms us, it reforms us, it rejuvenates us, it rescues us from unbelief, and it restores our heart for God. It takes our hurried hands and repositions them in a posture of hopeful communion with the Lord.

How about you pause for a bit and pray like your hurried hearts depended on it?

Part 3
Pursuit

By Brian Croft

CHAPTER SEVEN

Self-Care

There exists an incredible irony in the life of most pastors: they pour themselves out for the care of others—without regard for the need to care for themselves. When this happens, trouble is inevitable. A pastor's life will yield consequences—at times disastrous ones—when he breaches the boundaries of human weakness without giving proper attention to the need for rest and renewal.

While many humans experience stress, pastors experience a particular brand due to the spiritual nature of their calling. I have seen marriages implode, men break down mentally and succumb to deep depression, others suffer from stress-induced strokes and heart attacks, and even men end earthly life by suicide. A common thread connects every one of these tragedies—a neglect of personal soul care. This common denominator is pervasive among pastors despite the sobering warning that extends from the Israelites' example: "Let anyone who thinks that he stands take heed lest he fall" (1 Corinthians 10:12).

In the first two parts of this book, Ronnie has well captured the need to embrace our humanity, know we are weak, and seek an unhurried life of prayer, humility, and contemplation. Now it is time to consider how this is accomplished.

Unfortunately, pastors often get caught up in the overwhelming and unending pressures of the task of caring for others. Faithful pastors desire to shepherd God's flock as under-shepherds until Christ returns (1 Peter 5:2-4) and rightly seek to fulfill this calling sacrificially and diligently. The obedient pursuit of this calling, however, often results in an unwise inattention to their own soul, to the detriment of their health.

Paul, however, guides the Ephesian elders in the opposite direction when he gathers and exhorts them in Miletus before sailing for Jerusalem with an eye to reaching Rome. Luke records his counsel in Acts 20:25-32:

> And now, behold, I know that none of you among whom I have gone about proclaiming the kingdom will see my face again. Therefore I testify to you this day that I am innocent of the blood of all, for I did not shrink from declaring to you the whole counsel of God. Pay careful attention to yourselves and to all the flock, in which the Holy Spirit has made you overseers, to care for the church of God, which he obtained with his own blood. I know that after my departure fierce wolves will come in among you, not sparing the flock; and from among your own selves will arise men speaking twisted things, to draw away the disciples after them. Therefore be alert, remembering that for three years I did not cease night or day to admonish every one with tears. And now I commend you to God and to the word of his grace, which is able to build you up and to give you the inheritance among all those who are sanctified.

These Holy-Spirit-inspired marching orders establish one of the clearest models for pastoral ministry in all of Scripture. Verse 28 defines the pattern most succinctly: "Pay careful attention to yourselves and to all the flock." This single imperative—"pay careful attention"—constitutes the undeniable core of the Ephesian elders' work. While the cultural context for modern-day ministry is far removed from 1st-century Asia Minor, our central task remains the same.

Notice how Paul's charge to this group indicates two areas of focus:

1. Pay careful attention to yourselves.
2. Pay careful attention to all the flock.

Few, if any, pastors would dispute that the second admonition, to "pay careful attention ... to all the flock," sits at the center of our task as shepherds. Many pastors, however, are surprised to learn that the command to "pay careful attention to yourselves" is set equal to or higher than it. Grammatically, Paul places the call to keep watch over ourselves in the place of priority, making it a foundation for the second and more widely recognized one.

The aim of this chapter, then, is to consider the full range of Paul's first imperative, to "pay careful attention to yourselves." We'll consider what different areas need to be addressed in order for a pastor to care well for himself and the practical ways in which he can do so. The aim, as ever, is to bring joy, longevity, and sustainability to what can otherwise be a busy, hurried, and noisy ministry.

The Command and Its Meaning

The command to "pay careful attention to yourselves" is a warning for all pastors about the dangers of neglecting our spiritual health. Most directly, this verse warns about the hazards presented by false teachers, who promote false doctrine. Paul says, "And from among your own selves will arise men speaking twisted things, to draw away the disciples after them" (v 30). Lest any are lured into believing this is a hypothetical scenario, I could recount numerous tragic stories of this happening from personal experience. Even more, church history is replete with examples that illustrate the dire need for a pastor to watch out for himself—it is frighteningly easy to stray from the truth.

Looking elsewhere in the New Testament, we find Paul similarly exhorting Timothy to "watch your life and doctrine closely" (1 Timothy 4:16, NIV). The latter part of this succinct counsel addresses the necessity of giving careful attention to what he believes because this will inevitably steer what he preaches and teaches. But Paul speaks first to the character of the man and the manner of his life. Without exception, a pastor's ministry will be marked by how well his life matches the gospel he proclaims.

Our experience, however, is that there are additional layers to "pay[ing] careful attention to yourselves" that are vital for helping a pastor faithfully stay the course in the midst of a busy, frantic, hurried ministry life. Under the umbrella of this command, let's consider the spiritual, emotional, mental, and physical aspects of self-care that affect a man's ability to persist in this labor. We'll consider three things in particular: Engaging in spiritual soul care, embracing human weakness, and committing to personal self-care.[23]

Engaging Spiritual Soul Care

Spiritual soul care works itself out in three great loves.

A man devoting himself to the busy task of shepherding in the church—preaching, counseling, visiting, and leading—must first be transformed by the power of the gospel. This isn't a one-time event; he must continue walking in fellowship with Jesus every day. In recognition of his constant need for Jesus, he should be turning to him in faith daily through spiritual disciplines, especially prayer and Bible study. Through this Spirit-empowered pursuit of Jesus, the man knows and is known by him; he grows steadily in love for Jesus as he longs to experience intimacy with him. Confident that he is forgiven by Jesus, he cries out to him in moments of weakness and desperation, believing he is always heard. The bedrock relationship for any pastor is the one he has with his Savior. Being enslaved to an unsustainable ministry pace can be evidence of the absence of this crucial relationship in a pastor.

Growing out of, and supplying fuel for, his relationship with God, the pastor should also love God's word. God's word forms the foundation for all of life because only through it can we accurately know God and how we are to live in his world. Thus, the Bible is central to every aspect of our lives. Long before a man should ever presume to preach to God's people, he must devote himself to study the Scripture. Knowledge of the Bible, however, is not nearly enough. He must grow to love it by learning to feed on it, allowing it to nourish his soul.

Finally, the man who walks with Jesus and loves God's word must grow to love God's people. This third characteristic is both an outflow of the first two and a fruit of the Spirit. This genuine affection for God's people stimulates a commitment to sacrificially serve them, even at great cost, so that they come to know, love, and follow Jesus themselves. Love for God's people cannot be acquired by osmosis through formal processes like ordination, magically conferred along with a Master of Divinity degree, or even deposited along with a paycheck from a church. Instead, this love sprouts in the man who clings to Jesus as Savior and humbly submits to the transforming work of the Spirit by the word of God.

If reading this description leaves you feeling as though you have fallen woefully short in this area, take heart. All pastors fall short, but the abundant grace of God, which we encourage our people to receive and depend upon, is there in the same abundance for us! As we seek to know and follow Jesus in our shortcomings, it is in that precise fellowship with our Savior that we experience his mercy, accept his forgiveness, and are enabled to keep going. Ultimately, it is that forgiveness and mercy that empowers us to embrace our weaknesses.

Embracing Human Weakness

Strength in weakness is one the classic paradoxes of the Christian life. Worldly wisdom dismisses the idea that a person is strongest when they are weakest. Yet God delights in upending the wisdom of the world with his true wisdom. This concept is captured clearly in 2 Corinthians, where Paul refers to his request for God to remove a thorn in his flesh:

> But he said to me, "My grace is sufficient for you, for my power is made perfect in weakness." Therefore I will boast all the more gladly of my weaknesses, so that the power of Christ may rest upon me. For the sake of Christ, then, I am content with weaknesses, insults, hardships, persecutions, and calamities. For when I am weak, then I am strong.
> (2 Corinthians 12:9-10)

I have a confession to make. While always affirming Paul's teaching here as true, I have spent most of my life pretending that strength and weakness do not and cannot coexist. By God's grace, however, I am continuing to learn that this combination is a key for living courageously and in the freedom of the gospel. True strength comes from Jesus living in us, which requires our recognition of our weakness, sinfulness, humanity, and total dependence on him. Coming to grips with inability takes courage, but it is the only path to finding the divine strength necessary for faithful, pastoral ministry.

In earlier chapters, Ronnie reminded us that being human entails limitations, even as far back as Genesis 1 and 2—but ministering in our fallen world adds another layer of weakness. Paul reminds us here of the hardships and calamities he faces. So how do we acknowledge all these different areas of weakness and gain gospel-empowered strength? Consider these three realities.

First, we pastors must embrace the fact that we are sinners. While sin has been defeated and our bondage to it broken by the sacrificial death of Jesus, this freedom will not be fully realized until we are raised from the dead. Therefore, it is essential that we accept the weakness of our fallen humanity in this ongoing battle against sin. We are human, still wrestling with temptation and inevitably succumbing to it. This is by no means a call to embrace sin but to live in the reality of our need for Jesus' forgiveness. A denial of our proclivity to sin leads to failure and certainly not to spiritual strength.

Second, pastors must embrace the fact that we are not perfect; we cannot do everything as well as we'd like to. There are two sins in particular that pastors are prone to—perfectionism and an unhealthy love of control. But we are not God. Only God is perfect and controls the universe. We do not. Human weakness reminds us that we are not perfect nor in control. Perfectionism crushes the soul of a pastor and, many times, crushes the soul of those around him. Pastors love to declare the freedom they have in Jesus, yet many of these same pastors are crippled by a fear of failure. Devastated when they do not measure up to expectations set by themselves or by others, they respond with overwork or laziness. Some toil endlessly to live up to an unbiblical standard, while others slothfully despair until they give up.

I have great news: not one pastor is perfect. God never expects that we will do everything right. He knows we will fail, and he has already accepted us. God requires faithfulness of his servants, not perfection. To truly embrace our weakness, we must let go of the expectation of perfection and the illusion that we are in control.

Third, pastors must embrace the fact that we are physically frail. Pride can drive us to want to appear superhuman and unaffected by the realities of the fall on our bodies. We can keep pressing on physically in our hurried ministry life until we hit the wall. As Ronnie stated in an earlier chapter, part of embracing our weakness is the acceptance of our physical limitations. God has woven a rhythm of work and rest into creation, and pastors are not above it. We must learn to recognize when to work as well as when to stop and rest. This embrace of physical weakness leads naturally to the next area that helps us apply Paul's command to "pay careful attention" to ourselves.

Committing to Personal Self-Care

The rigors of a hectic ministry life lead many pastors to neglect the basic means of caring for themselves. Based on my experience over the years, I believe there are six areas of personal self-care that act as a gauge to ascertain when a pastor is struggling—and that, when attended to rightly, help a pastor to serve his congregation joyfully and sustainably. We will consider the first three in full in this chapter and then devote a whole chapter each to the final three.

Eat

We often rightly consider, "What do we eat?" or even "How much do we eat?" But I would argue that an equally important questions is "Why do we eat?" Allowing stress to drive us to eat or to avoid eating is evidence that a pastor is living under the pressures, demands, and stresses of his life and ministry in an unhealthy manner. So, how do we begin to work out whether we have a problem in this area? Here are four factors to consider.

First, grow in awareness. Without knowing what the real problem is, we cannot address it. Consider your family history and how you were taught to view and consume food. Was food a reward? Was food something used for comfort in difficult times in your home? Then, consider how you use food now. It was profound when I realized that food was a source of comfort for me in stress and anxiety. Until that realization came from God, I would just eat too much and not know why. The first step is to realize that the way we view and consume food can reveal much about our souls.

Second, keep a close eye on your weight. I once heard Pastor Al Martin address a group of pastors and share this simple but important truth: "What you eat and what is not burned off that day goes here, here, and here [referring to parts of his body]." My weight has become a very helpful gauge on how well I am doing in my battle against finding comfort in food. When my weight goes up, it could mean a number of things—yet what it most often exposes is that I am under more stress and eating more as a result. The managing of my weight becomes a gauge not just of stress level but how I am coping with it. If a pastor is 50 to 100 pounds (23-45kg) overweight, the cause may be a turmoil in the soul that cannot be ignored.

However, weight does not tell the full story. I once talked with a pastor who battled against overeating and yet was very skinny. He lamented how hard it was to battle with overeating and yet hear it often said, "You are too skinny. You need to eat more." Likewise, there are those who are overweight because of a thyroid or metabolism issue, not because they overeat because of stress. Despite these exceptions, our weight can tell us a lot. Keep an eye on it.

Third, care about your personal testimony. I'm not suggesting that a person who carries a bit of extra weight and doesn't exercise as often as they wished they did is in danger of marring their gospel testimony. Nor am I advocating that we are to somehow pursue an attractive exterior in order for our message to be heard. We are all broken vessels being used in the Master's hands. But, if a Christian is enslaved to any kind of substance—whether it be drugs, possessions, or food—it risks harming their testimony of the freedom we have in the gospel. Self-control is part of the fruit of the Spirit, which needs to be growing in our lives to affirm our testimony. The apostle Peter calls all pastors to be examples to the flock (1 Peter 5:3). Be mindful of your personal testimony.

Finally, find your comfort in Jesus. It is a powerful thing to realize, for example, that we use food as a means of comfort in this fallen world. But, the problem isn't stopped by mere awareness. Our souls are nurtured and cared for when we find comfort amid the stress and difficulties of ministry not in food but in Jesus. So let's run to him. Jesus satisfies in a way that even the best food cannot.

Pastors, be honest about the place food has in your life. It took me 30 years before I was honest about it. It will always be a battle for me—I continue to be tempted to soothe pain and sadness with food. But I also know that God's grace will meet me in that place of openness and honesty and will give me strength to walk in self-control and victory. He will meet you there too. He will work in your soul to bring the relief and peace that you truly seek.

Sleep

Many men have a problem with admitting to the amount of sleep they need because they wrongly understand the need for sleep as a sign of weakness. Biblically, however, we know that sleep is a necessary part of living as humans in God's world. This gift reminds us that we are not God, and it refreshes our bodies to allow them to function properly. Getting the proper amount of sleep is therefore essential to thriving as a human being—and as a pastor.

As with food, this is not merely a matter of the body. With pride, control, and confusion about godliness all in play, there is but one conclusion: this is a matter of the soul. So how does a pastor care well for his soul in regard to sleep?

We must first embrace our humanity, as Ronnie urged us to in previous chapters. One of the great differences between us and God is that we need sleep and he doesn't. So just be honest about how much sleep you need. I need eight hours. You may need nine hours when another pastor only needs seven. Until you embrace how God has made you as a human being who is weak and needing sleep, you will not be honest about how much you really need. But when we do embrace this, there is real freedom.

Second, we must acknowledge the gift of sleep. Sleep should not be seen as something we just need to do when we are too exhausted to do anything else. Sleep is a gift from God as a way to recharge and reset, so that we can be at our best to serve him the next day. Sleep is not a burden but a gift, and the pastor who acknowledges this will have a more peaceful soul.

Lastly, we must let go and trust Jesus. Sleep reminds us that, ultimately, we are not in control. When we lie down to sleep, we cannot escape that truth, even though we may have deceived ourselves all day about it. Pastors carry tremendous burdens throughout the day. What a gift it can be to relinquish those burdens to Jesus as we go to sleep.

I try to use my final moments before drifting off to sleep to say this prayer to God, aware of my own exhaustion:

God, I am reminded at this moment that I am not God. I am only human. I need sleep. I can't do anymore right now. But you are God. You don't need sleep. You are all-powerful and everywhere. This moment is a gift, as I get to sleep and let go of all these burdens I have carried for my people today. Help me to let go and give them over to you. Watch over me and my family tonight, for you are a God that doesn't sleep or slumber. May your mercies be new tomorrow. Thank you.

Pastors, sleep is a gift. Embrace it. Use it each night to unburden your soul and bring yourself some temporary relief. I assure you that there will be plenty for your soul to bear in the morning.

Exercise

The benefits of physical activity are varied and well documented. Of all these gains, perhaps most pertinent to pastors is that exercise presents one of the healthiest ways of dealing with stress, as well as one of the best strategies for avoiding unhealthy responses to stress such as overeating and overworking.

You may already acknowledge that exercise hasn't been in its proper place in your life. You even see the effects of its absence and know you need to make a change. And yet, this can feel like a daunting task, especially for pastors who did not grow up as competitive athletes and cannot rely on that muscle memory to kick in during adulthood. Here are a few ways to help you get started.

First, do something small to start with. Begin by going on a short daily walk in your neighborhood, perhaps with your wife. The pattern of inactivity needs to be broken, but it doesn't have to be through a goal like running a half-marathon next year. Just doing something begins to break the pattern. Set small achievable goals. Don't underestimate how something small in your regular daily routine will begin to bring the benefits God has designed us to gain from it.

Second, exercise with someone. This can be a great source of both motivation and accountability, especially for pastors trying to establish a habit for the first time. It would be ideal for a pastor to find another pastor who would commit to meeting three to four times a week at the gym or the park to exercise with you. As well as reaping physical benefits, you can act as a support and sounding board for each other in regard to ministry issues. I find it quite therapeutic to talk about ministry struggles while running, pounding out some pushups, or hitting a heavy bag.

Finally, commit long term. There's a reason the gyms of the world are packed the first week of January and return to normal six weeks later. Most people know exercise needs to be a part of their life, but fewer have the self-discipline and motivation to make it a part of their long-term lifestyle. It is crucial to a pastor's well-being that he implements a realistic exercise regimen in his busy life.

I know a 95-year-old widow who walks a track near her home three days a week. Just five years ago she walked five miles each time. Now, at 95, she still walks four miles each time. She is amazing. When I asked her how she was able to keep this up, she said this:

> I started a long time ago, and I have just kept doing it. There are many days I don't feel like it, but I know as soon as I stop, my body will slow down. The key is doing something for your whole life and sticking with it. It must be consistent, or it will never stick when you reach my age.

Pastors need to heed these words, not just for the sake of physical health but so that we can be our strongest to serve Christ in our calling. We have been given one body, and if we don't take care of it, it will hinder the noble work to which we have been called—both now and certainly as we age. Regular exercise will be a help to our bodies and is essential to the well-being of our souls.

Friendship

Ronnie and I are both convinced that friendship between pastors is the most commonly lost "piece" to persevering in ministry.[24] A pastor desperately needs friends, as does his wife. The unique calling of a pastor demands that we invest in relationships with other pastors because these relationships carry a sense of common understanding about our task. Such Spirit-empowered friendships not only encourage pastors but also, by extension, enable those under their care to flourish. More to come on this in a later chapter.

Rest

Because ministry never ends, pastors must find time to rest, be refreshed, and spend time away from the burden of their work. While connected to the daily need for sleep, this call to rest also includes a day off each week and regular vacation time. Yet resting requires more than time away from the church building and the cell phone. Pastors often fail to rest even during time off because they refuse to lay aside the mental and spiritual burdens of ministry. True rest requires entrusting people and their situations to God and allowing the heart and mind a respite from the weight of leading, feeding, protecting, and caring for the people. We'll explore this more fully in chapter 8.

Silence

Perhaps the best method of avoiding personal soul care is by filling our lives with noise, busyness, and distractions. If that is our tendency, we must find regular time for stillness, prayer, and quiet reflection. The spiritual discipline of silence and solitude is an instrument God uses to speak through his word, provide awareness of our pain and struggles, minister his grace, and give spiritual help in our time of need. We will return to this in chapter 9.

Blueprint for Joy

While these last three areas are being expanded on in upcoming chapters, it is important to see these six elements of self-care as one unit. They work together in tangible ways to nourish a pastor in body and soul, and to sustain him in ministry for the long term.

A frantic, hurried pastor will not care for himself. A hurried pace prevents it. Succumbing to the constant demands of others distracts from self-care. Only when a pastor allows himself to stop, be still, quiet, and unhurried, and give regular care to himself and his own soul, will he find the blueprint for thriving, experiencing joy, and serving Jesus over a long time in the ministry.

CHAPTER EIGHT

Rest

"What is it like to be a pastor?"

When I get this question from someone who has never been a pastor, here is my typical response:

> Being a pastor is like having 17 different tasks that have to get done today, but I only have time and energy to accomplish nine of them. So, every day is the hard choice of what to prioritize, what gets left undone, and who that will affect.

Additionally, the other factors often involved in that decision are the difficult reality of who gets upset over the undone tasks, what care for someone's soul didn't get ministered, and how that affects the to-do list for tomorrow. It is this scenario that often creates the frantic, hurried pastor and produces an environment in which pastors feel unable to ever stop and rest. This inability to rest is one of the greatest hindrances to the modern pastor.

I can relate. For most of my adult life, I didn't know how to rest. I was in too much of a hurry, trying to keep all the balls in the air. In fact, what I now understand to be rest and recreation I saw back then as laziness and lack of productivity.

After all, I thought, the kingdom of God is being built! Hurting souls need care. That sermon won't write itself. Who has time to rest?

But I eventually learned that every pastor needs to rest. I needed to rest. You need to rest. The hurried pastor may not be convinced he should rest, or that he can rest, but he needs to rest too. Otherwise, our souls are not given a space to breathe and recover from the grind and pace of ministry. I came to understand rest as essential. My hope is that you will too. This chapter will focus on three categories of rest in a pastor's life: a day off, vacation, and sabbatical.

A Day Off

Some like to question whether a pastor should take a day off. Let me be clear for those who are curious—yes! Every pastor should take a day off every week. Here are a few reasons why.

First, Sunday is a workday for a pastor. I know it is the Lord's Day. I know not all pastors preach on a Sunday. Regardless, while most are getting a break from their weekly grind on Sunday, the pastor is experiencing the pinnacle of it. Sunday is a joyful day, but it is also an emotionally draining day and is far from being low-key and restful.

Second, a pastor never really leaves work at the end of the day. Regardless of how we spend our evenings or how hard we try, the pastor never completely checks out. Even if the phone does not ring or no one stops by, the sermon is still on the mind and heart, and that elderly saint's battle with cancer still weighs on the shoulders. There is not a clock we ever punch that magically causes us to forget about the burdens of caring for souls until 9:00 a.m. the next morning. Although we can never leave the burdens, a day when we can step back, try to focus on something else, and escape the daily grind is invaluable for our souls and long-term ministry stamina.

Third, a pastor with children at home needs a weekly day when his family comes first and they know it. There are many sacrifices made by the pastor's family. Because of this, taking a day when children know they will be "dad's focus" helps them give dad up to the busyness of the other days. There are fewer more effective ways to communicate your love for your family than for them to know that there is a day for them, it is scheduled regularly, and, regardless of the craziness, it is coming soon.

A day off is also just as important for pastors who are single, married without kids, or older with grown children who are out of the home. In fact, the temptation for these groups to overwork is often greater, because they don't have children demanding their time. Regardless of whether little kids or a wife is waiting for you at home, the need to rest, unplug from ministry, and take a regular day off is just as essential for singles and empty-nesters.

One of the best decisions I have ever made for the benefit of my family and ministry has been to commit to a day off every week. Only funerals and true emergencies cause me to compromise it. My day off for most of my ministry was Friday because it fit best in our family schedule. Pick a day that works best for you and your family. The important thing is to pick a day, let your family and church know when that will be, and stick to it. I still manage to work about 50 hours a week with a day off. My family looks forward to it. Your family will too if you schedule it in your week and honor it. Little decisions like committing to a day off every week are crucial to the long-term care of your soul.

Vacation

Some of you reading this might be expecting me to suggest how many weeks of vacation you should be given by your church, or whether you should advocate for more. My concern is not about how much vacation time a pastor is given but how he uses (or doesn't use) what he is given.

This is an appropriate time to pause for a confession. I often fail to carry out my own advice. I do not write in this way because I have it all figured out. Far from it. The stewardship of my vacation time has been an area of glaring failure in my life, which I have tried to address in recent years.

Several years ago, I was lovingly confronted by a dear friend and fellow pastor about not using all my vacation time. In his rebuke, he explained to me the reasons why I should be taking every day of vacation the church gives me, which up to that point I had never done. Here is the basis of his thoughtful, insightful, and wise argument.

First, it's for you. An extended time away from work is essential to an unhurried life. The pastor never gets a break in the regular routine. We are constantly on call. Vacation time is an opportunity to get away from the madness and to breathe, be refreshed, and rest. All of us who are pastors know we are no good for our people when we are exhausted, distracted, and mentally and emotionally spent. Use the time and use it wisely to achieve those ends.

Second, he told me, it's for your family. Your family always has to share you. During vacation, your family has a blocked-off amount of time when they don't have to share you with the church. When you don't use all your vacation time—which has already been approved by the church for this purpose—you rob your family of being your sole focus in caring for, fellowshiping with, and enjoying them.

Third, it's for your church. How is it that many of our churches have existed and functioned just fine for the last 50 to 100 years without us? Yet, all of a sudden, we come up with this idea that our church can now no longer live without us for a week or two. Using all your vacation time forces others to step up in your absence, shows them they can make it without you for a time, and reminds the pastor most of all that God is not utterly dependent on him for this church to function. We are expendable, and we need regular jolts of humility to remind us of that.

Sabbatical

A practice common among some churches is to grant full-time pastoral staff occasional pastoral sabbaticals. During a sabbatical, a pastor sets aside regular pastoral duties (that is, preaching, teaching, leading collective worship, member care, and administration) to focus his time and energy on other profitable tasks.

I was given a sabbatical at the completion of ten years as senior pastor of my church. No pastor had ever taken a sabbatical in the 80-year history of our church. As a result, my fellow pastors felt a need to explain to the congregation what this foreign idea was. Here's the description they presented to our congregation:

> The intention of a pastoral sabbatical is to provide a time of rest, renewal, and refreshment of the pastor's soul and his family with longevity of ministry in mind. The pastoral sabbatical includes deliberate efforts for the pastor to grow, learn, mature, and excel all the more in his ministry upon his return. The pastoral sabbatical is distinct from vacation time. When the pastor uses vacation time, he is not expected to fulfill ministry obligations. However, during the pastoral sabbatical, the pastor is charged with engaging in devotional, theological, pastoral, and personal reflection and renewal.

A sabbatical can take on various form and lengths.[25] However it works, it should be seen as another layer of rest that is important for proper care of a pastor's soul and a healthy formula for a long, more sustainable ministry.

The Fight for Rest

The fight for rest in these three layers is real. The pastor must fight to see his own need for these kinds of rest and reject the lie that if he's not doing ministry in any given hour of the week, then he's being a bad steward of his calling. Additionally, there is pressure from the congregation that comes into play. "Is the pastor being lazy?" "Why does he need two to three months off when I only get two weeks?" The common result of these pressures is that the pastor doesn't rest. The hurried pastor just keeps going. And going. And going. Until he breaks and has no idea how he got there. Pastors, fight for your rest. Submit it all to the Chief Shepherd. Allow him to revive your tired and anxious soul.

One final warning. A pastor can consistently take a day off every week. He may use all his vacation time. He might even be gifted with a sabbatical from his church and use it. But that doesn't mean he is resting. The mindful unhurried pastor doesn't just embrace these tools of rest—he recognizes his need to let go of his ministry burdens when he rests. I know pastors who get more anxious on vacation than when at church because they are worried about what is happening while they are gone. I know pastors who take a sabbatical but never rest because they are tormented by their lack of control over what happens in their absence.

The unhurried pastor learns to let go. The unhurried pastor knows Jesus is the Chief Shepherd over his church. This pastor knows he needs to rest, and part of that rest is to have faith that Jesus will watch over his people in the pastor's absence. It requires faith for a pastor to let go and entrust his flock to the one whose flock they truly are—Jesus. It is only when a frantic, hurried pastor actually let's go that he truly rests.

CHAPTER NINE

Silence

I spent most of my adult life hating silence—and didn't know it. It was a major blind spot. I always dismissed my desire to be with people and avoid being alone as due to me being an extrovert and loving people. I excused my talkative nature as a sign of heightened relational instincts. These qualities also seemed to help my interactions with people as a pastor, so I thought nothing more of it. It wasn't until I began my own counseling journey out of a crisis that I was confronted with this long-held deception.

My counselor observed some behavior in my life that went unnoticed by most but became flags of concern for him. He saw that I ran from being alone. He realized I was uncomfortable in silence and didn't know how to face it. He experienced the way I often dominated conversations with my words. This also exposed my terrible listening skills. As a result, he began to press me in this area—and it was difficult.

Silence exposes the soul. Ugly things surfaced that I was not ready to face. At one stage it felt as though I had imploded. But God, in his amazing grace, met me in a sweet, powerful way and began a healing journey that has brought a consistent peace in my soul. It was only through silence that

I experienced this deeper level of God's grace and presence within my soul.

In order for a pastor to have a long and fruitful ministry, he needs regularly to experience the power and love of God in these deep places of his soul. These places cannot and will not be reached in the midst of the frantic, noisy, and distracted pace at which most pastors commonly live. Hurried pastors, by their very nature, run from stillness—but the practice of silence can be a powerful vehicle for renewal.

This chapter seeks to call every pastor to consider the discipline of regular silence and solitude, and to see how this could form an important part of the care of his soul. First, let's consider the reasons why silence can be beneficial and then turn to the practical question of how to begin to embrace it amid a busy and noisy ministry.

Reasons for Silence

Most of us can agree on some obvious reasons for silence: we all need time to get refocused, be alone with God, pray, and read God's word, free from distraction. However, I would like to give four additional reasons that may be less obvious—and that connect to silence being a catalyst for care for one's soul and for combating a noisy, hurried ministry.

First, silence exposes the soul. Busyness and noise are common defense mechanisms that we use to avoid pain in our lives. That could be unresolved pain and abuse from the past, or it could be current suffering. Regardless, noise and distraction can give the illusion that the suffering isn't there or that it has no power. Many pastors are in a hurried state, not ultimately to be productive but to run from the pain of their own soul. Silence can expose that deep pain and demonstrate its undeniable presence in our souls.

Second, silence confronts the voices; these voices are the messages we hear about ourselves, replaying in our mind. We all have them. They are the voices of people from our past. They are the lies the enemy loves to whisper in our ears. They are the messages of those currently in our life. When those voices are harsh and abusive, and they lie about our value and identity in Christ, they become very unpleasant to hear, and we do what we must to run from them.

For years, I was tormented by these voices. Abusive voices from my past, lies from the enemy, and painful words of criticisms from the present all created these messages of failure and self-loathing that were loudest when I was alone in silence. So, I ran from silence to try and escape these voices.

What I didn't realize, however, was that I needed silence in order to confront these voices. The solution wasn't to run from them but to speak at them: to speak powerful, gospel truth against the lies I had heard and believed for so long. Martyn Lloyd-Jones famously addressed these voices in the context of depression and said:

> The main trouble in this whole matter of spiritual depression in a sense is this, that we allow our self to talk to us instead of talking to our self. Am I just trying to be deliberately paradoxical? Far from it. This is the very essence of wisdom in this matter. Have you realized that most of your unhappiness in life is due to the fact that you are listening to yourself instead of talking to yourself?[26]

In order to do that, I needed space. Silence helped me to recognize the areas in which I was listening to myself instead of talking to myself. In silence I better identified the voices and was able to confront them with truth.

Third, silence teaches us to listen. It was troubling when I realized I had been a pastor for a long time and yet was such a poor listener. I listened, but it was to prepare to respond. I needed to learn to listen without a need to respond: to just listen and empathize. As I began to embrace silence, I realized I was beginning to listen too. I heard sounds around me that I had never noticed before. I felt more receptive to the message of God's word. It is amazing what happens when you are not so preoccupied with trying to figure out what to say or do next. Just listen.

Finally, silence tests our need for noise. I thought I just loved people and activity. I had no idea that I needed noise because my soul was tormented by silence. If you are a hurried pastor, it may be because you have an unhealthy need for noise too. Silence exposes the soul and can test how much we have grown to depend on noise to block out the pain of our lives. Pastors do not have to make much effort to find noise and distraction. It naturally flows from a hurried life. But silence is another matter. We must fight for it. Silence challenges us to face that pain and allow the power of the gospel to penetrate deep in our souls and bring healing. And yet, how does a pastor begin to embrace silence out of care for himself?

Embracing Silence

Once my counselor had identified my fear of silence, we started working on this together. Over a period of several months we set aside slots of time for silence. We began with 30 minutes and then expanded that to one hour. A half day of silence and stillness was the next big step. It all culminated in a silent retreat at a silent monastery, where I reflected back on what my time in counseling had taught me over the course of many months. When I arrived, I read these words on the wall:

> The role of silence was deemed to be important here,
> as a means of ensuring that one did not fritter away
> precious but demanding leisure through acedia [apathy]
> and small talk. Communities which respect human

growth probably need to make explicit provision for solitude; otherwise a potential source of enrichment is lost.[27]

Although I still hated silence, I had slowly come to realize that I needed to make "explicit provision for solitude" for the sake of my soul. My counselor had led me through a three-step process that helped me not just to realize that I needed silence but, eventually, to long for it. Since then, I have continued to practice these three "levels" of silence, and any pastor can follow a similar process: that process is daily silence, extended silence, and silent retreat.

First, a pastor can begin by practicing a short daily silence. Small but regular goals are the key. Don't underestimate the value of carving out five to ten minutes a day when you sit in silence with no music playing, no phone ringing, and no people talking. Just sit and take in the quiet. Be aware of God's presence. Listen to what is around you. I often do this on my back porch; I go outside and close my eyes, feel the breeze, hear the leaves rustle, and listen to the birds and animals move.

Most of all, receive God's grace as you ponder his favor and love towards you. After being still for the first few moments, you can begin to recite gospel truth to yourself. Center yourself with just you and Jesus, before you are bombarded by people during the rest of the day. Even if it is just five minutes of silence a day, I find this time invaluable when the rest of my day is full of people and noise. Five minutes each day is better than thirty minutes only once. These unhurried moments can be significant.

Next, a pastor needs to find more extended times of silence. This could be one hour a week when you are away from all noise and people to be alone with God. While daily silence helps keep me centered for the day, this extended time is what I find more restful and restorative. I typically do this on Monday mornings when I go running on a hiking trail away from people. After my run, I just sit in the quietness, aware of God's glory in creation all around me in the woods or near a pond. I remain still and know that he is God and that I am not (Psalm 46:10). For others, it might be a case of finding a quiet room in the house after the kids go to school. Whatever works for you, if you are intentional about scheduling this time in your week you will reap great benefits. If the daily silence keeps us going for the day, this extended time at least once a week is one means that God uses to restore our souls to him and remind us of his grace at work in us.

Finally, a pastor should move to scheduling one to two silent retreats each year. This could be an overnight trip somewhere, but it doesn't have to be. I have scheduled my silent retreats to be during the day; I will leave early in the morning and be back home for dinner. This pursuit of silence takes the care of your soul to another level for it exposes how much you need noise, people, busyness, and distraction. It will reveal how hurried you really are, and what exactly you are running from. My silent retreats have become a gut check on that which is hidden in my soul. Every pastor needs an opportunity to press into those hidden things, confront them before God, and stop and receive his grace and forgiveness.

My Silent Breakthrough

Over time, my counselor walked me through this three-step process. It led to the scary last step of a silent retreat. Although I had made some fruitful progress and developed a greater self-awareness of the activity of my soul, the prospect of this final step caused me much anxiety. After all, I hated silence because of the voices and messages that grew loud in that quiet place. I knew the enemy would be ready to try and sabotage my progress. Nevertheless, I took a needed risk and planned a whole day to go away and be silent before the Lord with my thoughts.

I wrote a lot that day in my journal. Here's an excerpt of my honest thoughts as I sat in that silent monastery alone:

I am sitting in a dead, eerie silence. I have always been terrible and terrified at silence. I always thought it was because of my personality. But I have learned that is not the case. I hated silence. Hated it. I didn't know why for so long, but now I do. Silence is where I was most tormented by the evil, abusive, and hateful voices of my youth. Silence is where the enemy shouted lies at me and I listened. Silence is where those messages of self-loathing came with a vengeance. Noise, busyness, endless chatter, and distraction muffled those voices. They distracted them to where I could tolerate them. But not in silence. There is no escape in the quiet. Silence is where they grew most powerful and attached to my identity with no way to stop their crushing affects. I hated silence.

This is why this day trip to a silent monastery was so scary. I know that I have been finding relief and freedom from these voices through the power of Christ and his truth at work in me this last year. But a place where silence is required may be the ultimate test. As I sit here, I realize it is. Even in the eerie silence of this beautiful place, the voices are silent. Their power to consume me in the past is what continues to be crushed by Jesus and the truth of his word. As I sit here, I realize not just the gift of silence and solitude, but how much I now love silence and long for it as a healing balm to my soul. Silence now reminds me of what Christ has set me free from and will act as that most helpful gauge to know and identify when these evil voices from the pit of hell are trying to return. If the Son has set you free, you are free indeed!

Jesus has set us free from the power of sin, shame, and death and has rescued us from the wrath of God, which we deserve. This is all by grace through faith. Our identity is now in Christ, and we are eternally adopted children of the one true God. We have the Holy Spirit of God indwelling each of us by faith, making us more like Jesus every day. And yet, so many Christians fail to experience the power of God's grace deeply in our souls. This includes pastors. That was me for most of my ministry, and it took an awareness of my own soul, and how to gain access to it, for the powerful grace of the gospel to permeate those deep, dark places.

Silence is a wonderful tool and gift from God to bring that awareness. We can only shepherd our people to the places where we ourselves have gone. Embrace silence as a peaceful, healing balm for your noisy, restless, and hurried soul. The hurried pastor could be using his busyness and hurried life to avoid his soul. But the unhurried pastor embraces silence and stillness as one of the most crucial tools to find the path to peace.

CHAPTER TEN

Emotions

Most of us are very familiar with the stoic, tough-guy masculinity that is traditionally taught to boys as they grow up. In its best form it is designed to produce hard-working, dependable, stable men who will support their family, contribute to society, and persevere through adversity. And yet, it remains a puzzling fact that rates of suicide are higher among men—those who have been trained to be tough and unshakable.

Here's how one secular writer tries to make sense of this inconsistency:

> Men are dying, dying in great numbers. It's a
> massive tragedy and it's going on under our noses,
> in our countries, our cities, our suburbs and in our
> neighborhoods ... We know from previous data that
> predominantly it is men (76%) taking their own lives,
> but what we don't tackle with enough willingness
> are the depths of the reasons why. It's not necessarily
> simple but a great start would be if we were to stop
> championing the aggressive, stoical form of masculinity
> that is embedded in society.[28]

It is safe to say that all men in our culture have been affected to some degree or another by this worldly version of masculinity in which real men don't cry. We are taught that real men are tough, stoic, unshakable, unmovable, self-reliant. Nothing is to rattle a man, and if it does, it is considered a sign of a weakness. What boy wasn't told after skinning his knee while playing in a game that he should rub some dirt on it and get back in there? What young man hasn't fought back tears when wounded out of fear of what his buddies might think? Whether your own father taught this type of masculinity or you saw it on the big screen, it is deeply embedded into the culture in which we live. This pressure to be the tough guy has ramifications other than the horrific reality of suicide for a few. An even more widespread tragedy is the way this form of masculinity paralyzes so many men's ability to love another person.

This false masculinity also exists in the church. Here in the US, many churches and seminaries wave the flag for hunting, flannel-wearing, steak-eating tough guys who shoot guns—and like it! In the UK, false masculinity might look like having a stiff upper lip and never showing any emotion. Other portrayals of masculinity are more nuanced, but nonetheless articulate a vision for manhood that only emphasizes one half of Scripture's full picture. To them, biblical manhood is *only* about initiative, leadership, and grit. These are indeed wonderful qualities in a Christian man. However, this limited focus leads to the neglect of a fuller understanding of biblical manhood, which includes tenderness, compassion, empathy, and love.

How should Christians process this type of one-sided, "tough-guy" masculinity—especially pastors? Here's a bold statement about this type of masculinity, which should inform our evaluation. It is a lie. It is unbiblical. There is no evidence in the New Testament that Jesus was stoic and unshakable. Quite the opposite. In addition to that, it is an unfulfilling way to live life. It hinders a man's ability to feel love and compassion for hurting people. And if that's the case, what happens to a pastor who embraces this worldly masculinity, yet is called emotionally and relationally to connect with hurting people? He is, at the least, less effective and many times risks harming people.

The pastoral call is to love: that is, to deeply empathize out of our own humanity and weakness, relate to the pain and suffering of others, and enter into their suffering. This cannot happen until the presuppositions we carry about being a "real man" get challenged at the soul level. But there is another important implication of this toxic understanding of manliness that speaks specifically to the frantic, hurried pastor. An inability to feel deeply keeps us in constant motion and encourages a busyness that, in turn, helps a pastor avoid the turmoil of his internal world.

This chapter seeks to help pastors confront this wrongheaded view of masculinity, which the world has sold us, to present a more biblical understanding of it, and then to help pastors begin to evaluate their own ability and their capacity to love and empathize. It is a pastor's ability to feel deeply that can ultimately lead to a more contemplative, present, unhurried life.

Feel Deeply to Love Deeply

God created us with emotions. Moreover, God created us with a whole range of emotions, and so there is a good and appropriate time for each of them: it's good to cry and feel sadness; it's good to allow yourself to feel anger; it's good to allow yourself to feel fear; it's good to allow yourself to feel hurt and frustrated. Our emotions remind us of our humanity.

Jesus, the perfect human, felt deeply too. The prophet Isaiah foretold that Jesus would be a man of sorrows acquainted with grief (Isaiah 53:3). Jesus felt righteous anger when he cleansed the temple (Matthew 21:12). Jesus experienced deep sadness when he wept at the tomb of Lazarus (John 11:35). Jesus endured fear and anguish as he prayed in the Garden of Gethsemane (Luke 22:44).

The Chief Shepherd feels deeply. So too are his undershepherds to feel deeply. Part of being an effective pastor is allowing ourselves to feel emotion and not be afraid of it. God made our emotions to be the gateway to our souls; it is through our emotions that we grow aware of what's going on inside.

And yet, a caution is needed as we allow ourselves to feel deeply. Paul instructs all believers to "be angry and do not sin" (Ephesians 4:26). Although we will experience real feelings of fear, Paul writes to his young protégé Timothy that God did not give us a spirit of fear (2 Timothy 1:7). Thus, it is also important that we are aware of the struggle with sin that can be manifested in these emotions.

Nevertheless, pastors are called to feel deeply so that we are able to love deeply. Paul taught that love is the core of the Christian life (1 Corinthians 13). Yet the tough, unshakable stoic cannot love deeply. A courageous pastor loves deeply and risks feeling deeply for others. Ultimately, it is the deeply feeling pastor who is able to stop, be still, feel with others, be present, connect on that human level, and minister God's grace.

Two Tests of Empathy

Most pastors intend to love deeply and sacrificially, but they may struggle to express that love in a way that can be received by others. So how can we tell if we're getting this right? Here are a couple of ways to test your soul's awareness and ability to love and empathize.

Test #1: Do you allow yourself to feel deep emotion?

There are many reasons that could keep a person from feeling deeply. First, it's worth saying that we are all wired differently, and we all have a different emotional "range" in which we operate, and that is ok. But some people only allow themselves to operate in a limited section of their emotional range because of the impact of negative experiences.

Here are a few of the most common examples I have observed in both men and women. First is the man who was taught that all emotion is bad and that it is unmanly to show it; emotion makes you less of a man and less of a person. It will give you the appearance of being weak and incapable. Second is the woman who's been told she's too emotional. So, she has dealt with this "problem" by doing whatever she must to control her emotions. Lastly, many people have experienced some trauma in their lives, such as abuse, which causes them to be afraid to feel deeply because the pain of those experiences is too much. In each of these three cases, individuals go throughout their life believing a lie—that emotion is bad. This does not magically change when a man finishes seminary or is handed the title of senior pastor.

The gospel of Jesus Christ can bring healing to our souls in such a way that in our new, born-again self we are able to feel deeply, empathize with suffering souls, and care selflessly for others. A restored ability to feel is one of many areas where the power of Christ through the Holy Spirit can take root and change us. It is in our weakness that Christ's power is perfected (2 Corinthians 12:9).

So embrace the gift of feeling deeply—and if there is something keeping you from being able to do this, begin to face it, knowing that Jesus can heal the most wounded, most suppressed heart. Allow other trusted pastors in your life to help you find healing in these areas. It may also be wise to find a trained counselor who could help you address some of the issues described above if you feel they have hindered your ability to feel.

Test #2: Are you able to experience compassion for hurting people?

It is an all-too-common mistake to confuse understanding with compassion. I assure you, there is a difference—experienced especially by the person on the receiving end.

Understanding means that we mentally acknowledge that a person is hurting and even see a justified reason for that. Compassion, on the other hand, allows us to empathize—to share the feelings of another. We don't simply acknowledge the hurt but experience the hurt with them. We truly bear the burden with them (Galatians 6:2). Herein lies a crucial difference.

When we interact with hurting people, our words, posture, tone, eye contact and countless other cues indicate whether we simply understand, or whether we actually empathize and bear the burden with them. Compassion allows a pastor to love and to feel for the hurting person more deeply and genuinely—and then, in faith, place that burden in the Lord's hand.

A Call for Emotional Courage

Churches don't simply need pastors; they need courageous pastors: men who are so secure in their identity in Christ that they are able to own their humanity, frailty, sin, weakness, and failures and remember they are loved and accepted by Jesus because of the gospel. This kind of pastor shows up as a loving and compassionate pastor; a humble and teachable pastor; a wise and discerning pastor, able to assess what is going on in his own soul and the souls of others. Pastors don't need to be perfect or have it all together. They simply need Jesus—and to know they need Jesus just as badly as everyone else. It is a courageous pastor who finds his strength in his weakness in such a way that he is able to care well for his own soul and the souls under his care.

The frantic, uber busy, and hurried pastor cannot be this kind of pastor. The hurried pastor is unable to stop, be present, and feel with others. Sadly, many pastors use busyness as the way to avoid their own emotions and to avoid empathizing with others. So take time to evaluate your own awareness of emotions. Do you feel deeply? Are you able to feel compassion for hurting people? Only the unhurried pastor is wise enough to know that if he desires to care well for hurting people, then he needs to slow down, be still, and feel.

CHAPTER ELEVEN

Friendship

Charles Spurgeon (1834–1892) is one of my heroes. I admire many of the same things about him that others do: his Christ-centered preaching, wit, humor, courage, authenticity, boldness, brilliance, and ministry faithfulness, to name a few. However, the more I learn about this "prince of preachers," the more I feel drawn to some of the lesser-known qualities of this larger-than-life figure. Among these was his commitment to close, intimate friendships with other men—particularly pastors.

Author Iain Murray wrote a biography of Spurgeon's eventual successor, Archibald Brown (1844–1922). Before taking over Spurgeon's congregation, Brown pastored another large congregation on the other side of London from Spurgeon. There are a few moments in the book when Murray beautifully captures the sweet friendship that existed between Brown and Spurgeon. For instance, when Brown suffered the loss of his second wife, just a few years after his first, Spurgeon cared for him in the midst of his despair. Writing later, Brown recalled:

Broken with sore grief, I went over to the Metropolitan Tabernacle. I could not preach, but I thought I could worship, and how amazed I was to find that he had prepared a sermon on purpose for me ... As I turned round to come out at the close of the service, there was just one grip of his hand as he said, "I have done all I can for you, my poor fellow." I felt he had. I rode home with him that day, and had his loving fellowship as he sat with me during the afternoon.[29]

Years later, when Spurgeon was just a few weeks from his own death, he penned this final letter to Brown:

Beloved Brother, receive the assurance of my heart-love, although you need no such assurance from me. You have long been most dear to me; but in your standing shoulder to shoulder with me in protest against deadly error, we have become more than ever one. The Lord sustain, comfort, perfect you! Debtors to free and sovereign grace, we will together sing to our redeeming Lord, world without end.[30]

After Spurgeon's death, Brown spoke emotionally about his dear friend in his sermon the following Sunday:

He has been to me a very Elijah, and I have loved in any way possible to minister to him. Our roots have been intertwined for well nigh thirty years. Is it any wonder that I feel almost powerless this morning to think of him as a preacher, as an orator, as an organizer, or as anything except the dearest friend I have ever known.[31]

Spurgeon and Brown were spiritual giants of their day, pastoring two of the largest churches in all of England. And yet, they both knew there was something they needed in order to survive the noisy, busy rigors of ministry and the personal suffering of their life—friendship. Not just any friendship but a close, personal, intimate, and sacrificial pastor-to-pastor friendship, in which each regularly turned the other's gaze to Jesus.[32]

This chapter seeks to persuade every modern pastor of their essential need of this kind of friendship. It is a need that touches the deepest parts of the human soul, pastors included. And it is a need that is not simply rooted in enjoyment and companionship but in caring well for one's soul and surviving a long-term ministry. Pastoral friendship is an oft-forgotten piece of a persevering ministry, and it is only a contemplative, humble, unhurried pastor who will acknowledge this need and take the time to invest in it.

What Is Friendship?

Let us start with a basic definition: friendship is an intimate relationship of love, trust, and loyalty.

Here are a couple of additional observations as you think about this definition. First, the deepest experience of friendship will happen between those who know and follow Jesus. That's not to say that we can't have meaningful friendships with unbelievers—we certainly can. But there are natural limitations to the closeness of those relationships.

Second, you may have noticed a certain word choice that makes some men uncomfortable. The phrase "intimate relationship" was carefully chosen. Many in our cultural moment—both secular and Christian—have wrongfully positioned the word "intimate" to exclusively imply sexual connection. That can be an aspect of intimacy, but if we dig into the basic definition of "intimate," it speaks of "a warm friendship developing through long association."[33] This is precisely the kind of friendship that frantic, busy pastors desperately need and benefit from immensely; and it is the kind of friendship highlighted in the relationship of David and Jonathan in 1 Samuel 23.

The Context of 1 Samuel 23

1 Samuel 23:1-15 finds Saul as king of Israel and David on the run from him. Saul is pursuing David to kill him. Regardless, David continues to hear the voice of the Lord and does what he commands, defeating the Philistines in Keilah by God's hand (v 1-5). When Saul hears of this, he decides to come after David, thinking he will be able to trap him in the city (v 10-12). God tells David that the people of Keilah, whom he has just rescued, are going to turn against him and surrender him to Saul. This forces David to run again, and by verse 15 he is tired, weary, afraid, and doubting God as he hides in the wilderness of Ziph. But that changes when a friend shows up—Jonathan.

The Need for Friendship

David is not a pastor. This is not the church. However, there are some principles from this passage that can and do apply in the life of a pastor. Some of David's challenges resonate with us. Perhaps you know what it is like to serve in an environment where not everyone likes you, is for you, and wants good for you. In fact, we need friendship for at least these three key reasons.

First, we need friendship because ministry leaders inevitably experience opposition. If you want everyone to like you, don't lead. Opposition is a reality for every leader. Admittedly, the king pursing you to kill you is on another level! But Saul's hatred for David reminds us that every leader, in the face of opposition, needs to know someone is for them.

Second, we need friendship because ministry leaders will experience betrayal. I remember early in my ministry reading a startling Spurgeon quote that started with "When your brother betrays you…" I thought, "Don't you mean 'If…'?" Two months after reading that quote, I experienced one of the most painful ministry betrayals of my life. David defeated the

Philistines to save the people of Keilah, only to find out that they would give him over to Saul at their first opportunity. In a similar way, it is often these sheep that a pastor seeks to care for that bite him. This creates a distinctive kind of loneliness for leaders that is combated by meaningful friendships.

Lastly, there is a need for friendship because ministry leaders are tempted to doubt God in suffering. The Lord protected David and guided him every step of the way. But that didn't make things easy. David continued to flee Saul as Saul sought him every single day (v 14). Imagine the toll it must have had on David, to constantly be on the run, weary, lonely, and wondering what God was really doing in all this. While our circumstances may be less extreme, busy, frantic pastors can experience a similar type of toll—especially if they deal with the suffering in their lives and ministries by distracting themselves with yet more work, noise, and hurry.

The Benefits of Friendship

Jonathan arrives at the perfect, providential time for David, who desperately needs a friend. Their short, climactic interaction powerfully captures some of the benefits of friendship:

> *15David saw that Saul had come out to seek his life. David was in the wilderness of Ziph at Horesh. 16And Jonathan, Saul's son, rose and went to David at Horesh, and strengthened his hand in God. 17And he said to him, "Do not fear, for the hand of Saul my father shall not find you. You shall be king over Israel, and I shall be next to you. Saul my father also knows this." 18And the two of them made a covenant before the LORD. David remained at Horesh, and Jonathan went home. (v 15-18)*

First is the benefit of presence (v 15-16). Jonathan "rose and went to David." Don't miss the power of that gesture.

David is running from Saul, and it is Saul's own son who runs to David. Never underestimate the power of presence. Sometimes all we need when it feels like everyone is against us is a friend to simply be present and remind us that someone in this world is on our side.

Second is the benefit of strength (v 16). The writer specifically highlights that Jonathan "strengthened [David's] hand in God." We are not told exactly what that entailed. It could mean a lot of things. But the point is that God used Jonathan to strengthen David's weary hand for the tasks ahead, in a way that only Jonathan could do.

Third is the benefit of comfort (v 17). Jonathan says, "Do not fear." This implies that David was afraid and that Jonathan saw that he was afraid. Despite Jonathan being Saul's son, he couldn't prevent Saul's army from coming after David. That's not the point. It is the calm and comforting words of a friend to say, "Don't be afraid. I'm here with you and so is God—and he will accomplish all that he intends."

Fourth is the benefit of protection (v 17). Jonathan says, "The hand of Saul, my father shall not find you." This alludes to his own desire to do what he can to protect David at all costs from his father, but it also points to a confidence in God's protection of him. Sometimes we need the voice of a friend to simply say, "If Saul comes after you, he will have to come through me first." I remember having such a friend in the early years of my pastoral ministry as I served in a hostile environment. It made all the difference that someone was with me like that.

Fifth is the benefit of providence (v 17). Despite the suffering that David is enduring—which is enough to make any leader doubt God's plan—Jonathan reminds David of God's purposes in all this: "You shall be king over Israel, and I shall be next to you." Saul's pursuit has not changed God's providential plan for David—he will still be king. Sometimes we need a friend to enter into our suffering and remind us that God is not caught off guard in the same way that we are. In fact, our suffering is a part of his mysterious hand working his purposes in our life.

Lastly is the benefit of promise (v 18). Jonathan seals his strong, comforting, and providential words to David with a covenant. Jonathan and David "made a covenant before the LORD"—a binding agreement between two people before God. While we may not typically make such covenants these days, meaningful friendship must still be built on trust and dependability, and will often involve coming before the Lord together. David and Jonathan's actions in this moment is a helpful example of how good friends can jolt us out of our frenzied ministry lives and help us to be still and wait on the Lord.

Pursing Meaningful Friendships

The problem with pastors and friendships is we are usually too busy and hurried to cultivate them. There is no short cut to finding meaningful friendships, but for those pastors willing to invest the time and effort, here are three tips as you do that:

1. Value the power of presence

Most people assume that friendship is about a relationship with someone that is based on interactions, conversations, advice, wrestling through struggles, and talking through solutions. This is certainly assumed in the area of pastoral friendships, where we tend to seek relationships with other pastors to help ourselves wade through the tricky waters of church ministry. But sometimes what we need is a friend who is willing to simply sit with us, be present, and listen.

One of the most important friendships in my life is a weekly coffee meeting I have with a fellow pastor every Wednesday morning. The sole focus of this time together is for us to care for one another's soul. We rarely talk about ministry problems. We don't hash out solutions to church challenges. We don't discuss the sermon series we are preaching. We talk about each other. We check in on our emotional state, mental capacity, and spiritual engagement. Nothing is off limits. We can bring whatever we need to bring to each other, and there is no judgment. We come together to assess the activity of our own souls before God. We best accomplish this through a single commitment to one another—presence. We are committed to come together and simply sit with one another. Sometimes one of us shares more than the other. But our commitment is to sit and listen and be present to the need of the other.

Sometimes our most meaningful friendships are not those relationships where we come together to intensely dialogue but those relationships where we simply enjoy the presence of the other—even if that's sometimes sitting in silence together. That's what this friend is to me. And our friendship is special. There is a time to speak, yes, but with many pastors already having to navigate a number of voices in their life, I assume all pastors would be better equipped to persevere in ministry if they had friendships that involved fewer words and warmer presence as their foundation.

2. Seek friendships inside and outside the church

While the value of friends in the same ministry trench cannot be overstated, the addition of friends outside our particular ministry field is also important. Time and distance make these relationships more difficult to develop and maintain, but they sustain a pastor, and his wife, in critical ways.

Some of my most meaningful pastoral friendships to this day were found outside my church context, but one of the most crucial friendships developed outside my church with someone who wasn't even a pastor. As I pastored a local church and led a growing ministry to other pastors,[34] I found myself always surrounded with those who wanted me to be their pastor. I had church members looking to me as their pastor. And I had other pastors looking to me as a kind of pastor to them. I reached a point of exhaustion when I realized I needed a meaningful relationship with someone who didn't want me to pastor them.

My wife had felt the same need and had developed a meaningful friendship with another woman in our city, not a pastor's wife, who went to church across town. Her husband was a Chick-fil-A owner/operator and was a faithful church member. Having been at some group gatherings with him as a result of our wives' friendship, I reached out to see if he might want to spend some time together.

Over time, we developed a very meaningful friendship. He didn't want to talk about ministry. He didn't want to talk much about church stuff or theology. He wanted to eat hot wings, watch some football, talk a little politics, and share about our families. We talked about hobbies, other interests, and our own walks with the Lord as men. God used this friendship to show me two things about myself. First, how refreshing this friendship was to all my other relationships. Second, how much I needed a friendship like this to provide an environment of rest from all the other ministry and related relationships that had consumed my life. His friendship is still incredibly important to me.

3. Pray for each other

One of the simplest and most fruitful contributions we can make to our friendship is to pray regularly for our friends—as we do so, God will use our prayers to stir love and loyalty in our hearts for them.

When I consider those pastoral friendships that mean the most to me, that isn't gauged by how much time I spend with them or how much they have sacrificed for me. It is based more on their intentional efforts to pray for me when I least expect it. I remember a season of being overwhelmed with ministry that created a deep sense of loneliness. I found myself asking, "Does anyone actually care about me, or do they only want something from me?" In a very low moment while driving down the road, I received an unexpected phone call from a friend. I answered and he said, "Hey, I don't need anything from you, I was just thinking about you and wanted to know how you were doing, tell you that I love you, and ask how I could pray for you."

I began to weep while driving down the road, and I had no idea why. I realized later that I was deeply longing for someone not to need anything *from* me but simply to care *for* me. I learned something important about myself that day, but I also learned what I need in pastoral friendship—being loved for who I am, not what I can do. In my work supporting other pastors, I have learned that this is a deep longing shared by many whose calling is to pour out so much for others. This longing can, in part, be filled with meaningful, reciprocal pastoral friendships.

This experience also created a desire in my heart to be the same friend to others as this friend had been to me that day. As a result, much of my ministry rhythm has become one of sending random text messages to pastor friends and calling others on the phone when they least expect it, to say, "I love you. I was thinking of you. And I wanted to know how I could pray for you."

We all need friends. But pastors who are stuck in the frantic pace of ministry, thinking people only want them for what they can do for them—they especially need friends. The unhurried pastor stops and takes the time to consider their need for care and invests in the types of meaningful pastoral friendships where that care is found. Friendship is precious, but every pastor must carve out time from the demands of his schedule to cultivate it.

Spurgeon and Brown needed each other. David and Jonathan needed each other. And every pastor who seeks to find a joyful, enduring ministry needs safe, honest, meaningful friendships too.

Doing Less to Accomplish More

We commend you for making it this far.

However long it took you to get here, you stopped, read, contemplated, and considered our desire to redefine your understanding of ministry productivity. Regardless of where you go from here, that is "unhurried" progress to become a more "unhurried pastor." Well done.

But we must face reality. Reading about how to redefine ministry productivity is one thing, but making the necessary changes in order to function that way is another. Reading about our humanity and weakness and the need for self-awareness is one thing, but embracing them as we face the pressures of ministry is quite different. Reading about rest, contemplation, silence, and friendship sounds right, but actually doing them is another matter.

And yet, we believe that becoming an unhurried pastor is worth it: the benefits of an unhurried ministry far outweigh the work it takes to unlock them. Therefore, we encourage you to take yet another step away from your frantic, busy, hurried ministry life with a final plea to consider just three of these benefits: joy, effectiveness, and longevity. We hope these will motivate you to continue pursuing a more unhurried pattern of ministry.

Joy

An unhurried pastor experiences more and deeper joy from the ministry. The frantic pace of the busy pastor often steals the joy of the work. Many pastors are too caught up in the rat race to stop and smell the roses. What we have written about in this book, if embraced, will lead to a more joyful experience of leading your church and shepherding the souls of God's people. Joy comes when we embrace who we are in Christ, not just what we do. Joy comes from unhurried presence, not constant motion. Be motivated to press on in this soul work because you desire to truly enjoy your calling and labors in your ministry.

Effectiveness

An unhurried pastor is a more effective pastor. We have addressed how counterintuitive this concept is. Clearly, to be productive and most effective, we need to be busy, right? Nope. We hope we have at least challenged that understanding of ministry effectiveness in your mind, and also challenged you to reconsider what it means to truly be fruitful in your pastoral work. An unhurried pastor cares for himself, embraces his humanity, and focuses on *being* as well as *doing*. We believe that is the formula not just to experience more joy but to be most full and fulfilled, so as to be ready to pour oneself out for the good of others. Carry on in this pursuit of a present-focused, contemplative, unhurried life and trust that God will bring kingdom fruitfulness in your ministry.

Longevity

An unhurried pastor has the best chance of being a pastor for a long time. He understands that the call of God—leading a local church, ministering God's word, and caring for hurting souls—is a marathon, not a sprint. He realizes that his task is to sow the seed and wait for the seed to find good soil, sprout from the ground, grow, and then bear fruit much later (Mark 4). He knows the kingdom of God is built slowly, subtly, and in hidden, mysterious ways. The pastor who embraces the call to be more than do, will be more able to continue for a long time. In contrast, the perpetually hurried pastor inevitably burns out eventually. Be motivated to continue this soul work of cultivating patience and perseverance so that you may finish well what you started.

Brothers, allow the prospect of joy, effectiveness, and longevity in the ministry to motivate you to let go of your hurried manner of ministry and embrace this alternative approach. It is an approach that Eugene Peterson prophetically saw, embraced, and modeled, and now calls this next generation to walk in. He did so that we too might experience the joyful, thriving, and persevering ministry he discovered and that God desires for each of his undershepherds.

So then, since we started with the voice of Peterson, we will allow him to have the final word:

> There is a paradox here: the less busy we are, the more
> free we are to do the essentially Christian acts. The less
> we hassle ourselves and one another with jobs, lists, and
> endless moralistic house cleaning, the more focused
> we become for truly productive lives of creation and
> vocation. The less we do, the more we find our Lord the
> Spirit doing in and through us.[35]

Do less so that you might accomplish more for Christ and his kingdom.

Daily Spiritual Health Plan

BY RONNIE MARTIN

This daily spiritual health plan is designed to create new rhythms that cultivate healthier leadership patterns. Although these rhythms can be difficult to start—perhaps because of the vulnerability, unfamiliarity, and discomfort they initially surface—when exercised regularly, pastors will develop a spiritual "muscle memory" that will lead to a lifestyle that avoids burnout over the long term. Slow but steady consistency is key.

The emphasis of the Daily Spiritual Health Plan is what we called in chapter 6 "productivity of the heart." Without realizing it, pastors can develop an imbalanced focus on cultivating "productivity of the head and hands," while neglecting the more foundational work of the heart. The Daily Spiritual Health Plan, therefore, will help pastors place a renewed emphasis on the "productivity of the heart" and then use that as a measuring rod for how they approach the "productivity of the head and hands."

The Daily Spiritual Health Plan offers detailed spiritual exercises that cover the three main "movements" of the day: morning, afternoon, and evening. The aim is not to add another "thing" to accomplish in an already busy life but to see that the most important function of the Christian life is to become a more deeply formed image-bearer of Christ.

As a note of caution, the Daily Spiritual Health Plan should not be approached the way many do a diet plan—that is, as a set of rules that needs to be followed rigidly in order to achieve the desired results. The Daily Spiritual Health Plan is not so rigid that if one movement is missed, then the whole plan collapses. Instead, approach the plan as a way of providing new spiritual rhythms for the heart, which can develop a healthier pulse, which, by God's grace, may inform everything done in both ministry and life.

Morning reminder: The beginning of your days come with unexpected challenges, a variety of diverse time constraints, and a multitude of physical, emotional, and spiritual realities. These make every morning a unique experience in your spiritual journey with Jesus. Remind yourself that none of these things are unknown to him and that he will not be angry with you for failing to conform perfectly to a schedule that he didn't personally design. This spiritual health plan is not meant to give you another way to fall short but a smorgasbord of opportunities to get to know yourself and to know Jesus more fully. This morning communion is a way to take inventory of the productivity of your heart, so that the goal of productivity of your head and hands doesn't lead you down a path of manic activity and unrealistic expectations. These morning habits are designed to heighten your sense of awareness of both yourself and God.

Your Morning Communion
(Spend 15-60 minutes every morning before departing for work.)

Reflect
If you can, find a quiet place where you can experience uninterrupted solitude and some beauty. This is a time to let the Holy Spirit sort out your head and speak to your heart.
- *Presence: Where are you? Where is God?* (See Genesis 3:9.) Truthfully identify your feelings and what you believe God's response to be as you express them.
- *Listening: What is your body doing right now?* (See Psalm 63:1.) Be honest about the physical state of your body— what hurts, what's weary, what's going on in your gut, etc.
- *Contemplate: Identify your inner dialogue / what is God saying to you?* (See Psalm 85:8-9.) What was the first thing you thought of when you woke up? What

thoughts are cycling through your mind? How does God's truth connect with these thoughts? As you process them, what might he be saying to you?

Receive

As the day's worries begin to surface and stir, let yourself fall into the word and prayer. Visualize this exercise as a meal with Jesus himself, like that from John 21, where he made Peter and the disciples breakfast.

- *Reading: Daily reading of God's word.* Immerse yourself in God's word by continuing whatever daily reading plan you already have in place.
- *Prayer: Pray through a psalm.* Cycle through the Psalms by reading one a day, and use them as the foundation for beginning your morning prayers.

Respond

Having spent time reflecting and receiving from the Lord, respond to him in gratefulness, acknowledging that he has delivered you from the domain of darkness and that he is for you. Let your heart become glad in the Lord and in awe of his beauty and majesty.

- Speak or write about 1-5 things about God that you are grateful for (see Psalm 8).
- Speak or write about 1-5 blessings that you are grateful to God for (see Psalm 9:1).
- Speak or write 1-5 prayers that God has answered (see Psalm 4:1).
- Speak or write one promise that God has given you in Christ (see 2 Peter 1:4).

Recreate

Many pastors and church-planters have the flexibility to make changes, move dates around, and edit their schedules in order to create good margins.

- One thing you can remove today (to create better margins)
- One thing you are looking forward to (to create hopeful anticipation)
- One thing you can plan for today or for the future (to create organizational clarity)

Afternoon reminder: By this point, you have likely reached a point where you are mentally and physically weary. Though you are only at the halfway point of the day, it is beginning to feel long, and perhaps you are anticipating the hour that you can return home. Discouragements may have surfaced: a critical email from a particular church member, a sticky confrontation with a staff member, someone's struggles that are keeping your thoughts in a tangle, or a difficult sermon text that has you feeling anxious and unsettled.

Many of us spend time with Jesus in the morning only to move into a "work mode" mentality that has us relying solely on ourselves to survive the rest of the day. By taking a few precious minutes to pause and recenter yourself, you acknowledge both your limitations and the unlimited love and care that is waiting for you as you reengage with Jesus, who is Lord over every afternoon.

Don't forget to listen to your body during this time of the day too. Are you hungry? Are you properly hydrated? Don't neglect these important pieces!

Your Afternoon Contemplation
(Spend 10-30 minutes before returning to work/office.)

Recenter
You were not created to be a machine in a factory; your body requires healthy space and pace in order to function well. While most pastors will have a hard time recentering themselves, do your best to make it a priority so that you can experience the benefits it provides.
- *Find a place where you can experience a moment of solitude* (Mark 6:31). Try to find a quiet place to spend time intentionally reconnecting with the Lord.
- *If you are able to, close your eyes for 10-20 minutes* (Psalm 127:2). A short afternoon siesta helps you to renew, reenergize, and refresh.

Reflect

Repeat the steps from your morning communion:

- *Presence: Where are you? Where is God?*
- *Listening: What is your body doing right now?*
- *Contemplate: Identify your inner dialogue / what is God saying to you?*

Recall

Even though you spent time with Jesus this morning, the pressures of ministry and the work of the enemy threaten to move you into a state of forgetfulness. Spend time recalling the beauty of Christ, his secure hand in your life, his promises to never leave or forsake you, and his sovereign control over every tiny detail of your life.

- *Close your eyes and take some slow, deep breaths.* These types of exercises can help relax your body and mind and help you refocus.
- *Reflect on a Scripture passage you read during your morning communion.* The Lord spoke to you this morning, so take a moment to recall his words and how they might be speaking to you this afternoon.
- *Pray a short prayer praising God, thanking him for his mercy and grace and offering a petition.* This is how we "pray without ceasing" (1 Thessalonians 5:17). We learn to have an ongoing dialogue with our Savior, recalling his greatness, being thankful, and voicing our requests, as he has asked us to.

Reengage

Returning to the productivity of your head and hands can be challenging at this time of the day. By recentering your heart, you can enter back into your work with an awareness of your limitations and a gratefulness to God for the work he will sustain you to complete.

Evening reminder: The end of your day can produce a mixture of exhaustion, relief, discouragement, frustration, accomplishment, gratefulness, joy, and satisfaction depending on a multitude of factors. Returning home after a long day of ministry can reveal a pastor, husband, or father who is not at his best but who needs to engage with his family, who have been anticipating his return. It is important at this time of the day to have compassion on yourself and to remember that whatever lies unfinished can be accomplished tomorrow. The Lord knows that you are physically and mentally tired, that the day is still far from over, and that you are limited in what you have to offer your family, friends, and church members. See yourself through the eyes of your Savior, who wants you to find rest in him in your weariness, while offering you endurance to engage in the rest of your day with joy.

Your Evening Commencement
(Spend 10-30 minutes before you arrive home or before bed.)

Recount
Think back on the day and recount God's wondrous deeds in your life and the life of the church. Our tendency is often to focus only on the difficult moments of the day and so miss the good that God worked in and through us, and how he drew close to us amid it all.

- *How did you see God move in you, around you, and through you today?* Take some time to open your eyes and see how God moved.
- *Speak, write, or share one joy—physical, emotional, or spiritual.* Search your heart for a joy that God gifted to you. Some days this will be harder than others!
- *Speak, write, or share one low—physical, emotional, or spiritual.* Difficult moments should be acknowledged so that you can bring them to the Lord in honesty.

Resist

There is a temptation at the end of the day to collapse in a heap of exhaustion and discouragement. Resist the temptation to either check out or be in a bad mood by reaffirming who Jesus is and who you still are because of your identity and security in him. You are not your ministry!

- What truth about God do you need to be reminded of? (See Psalm 103:13.)
- What lies about yourself are you believing tonight? (See 1 Peter 2:9-10.)

Rest

Depending on your stage and season of life, rest may have to be fought for! But it is the worthiest of aims. This plan is not designed to tell you what kind of rest is best for you but to encourage you to set aside your busy work and give the Holy Spirit space to replenish your soul.

- What are you thankful for tonight?
- What can you trust God for as you reflect on what remains unfinished?
- Before bedtime, pray a short prayer of adoration and confession.

Endnotes

1 The Barna Group, https://www.barna.com/research/pastors-quitting-ministry/ (accessed Nov. 8, 2023)

2 https://expastors.com/why-do-so-many-pastors-leave-the-ministry-the-facts-will-shock-you/ (accessed Nov. 8, 2023)

3 https://pirministries.org/wp-content/uploads/2016/01/FASICLD-Statistics-on-Pastors.pdf (accessed Nov. 8, 2023)

4 Brian Croft serves with Practical Shepherding. Ronnie Martin serves with Harbor Network. Both of these roles focus on the care of the pastor and his family in the midst of the unique challenges of pastoral ministry.

5 We would acknowledge that we both have significant differences in ministry philosophy, theology, and practice with Peterson. Despite this, we both agree that Eugene Peterson's voice was incredibly undervalued, and the way he pushed against the accepted busy, noisy, frantic ministry practice of the modern age was essential and unmatched. Winn Collier's most recent biography on Eugene Peterson, *A Burning in My Bones*, is a beautifully written account of Peterson's life and one we highly recommend for further study.

6 Eugene H. Peterson, *The Contemplative Pastor: Returning to the Art of Spiritual Direction* (Wm. B. Eerdmans Publishing Co., 1989), p 19.

7 As above, p 20-23.

8 Joseph A. Fitzmyer, *The Gospel According To Luke X-XXIV* (Doubleday Publishing Group, 1985), p 892.

9 Darrell L. Bock, *Luke Volume 2: 9:51-24:53* (Baker Academic, 1996), p 1040.

10 As above, p 1042.

11 Joel B. Green, *The Gospel of Luke* (Eerdmans Publishing, 1997), p 436.

12 As above, p 437.

13 As above, p 437.

14 John Nolland, *Word Biblical Commentary, Luke 9:21-18:34 Volume 35B* (Thomas Nelson, 1993), p 605.

15 John Calvin, *Institutes of the Christian Religion* (Banner of Truth, 2014), Introduction.

16 Brevard S. Childs, *The Book of Exodus*, p 330.

17 Thomas B. Dozeman, *Exodus*, Eerdmans Critical Commentary (Eerdmans Publishing, 2009), p 408.

18 T. Desmond Alexander, *Apollos Old Testament Commentary: Exodus* (InterVarsity Press, 2017), p 354.

19 Robert Robinson, "Come Thou Fount of Every Blessing" (1758).

20 Martin Lloyd Jones, *Preaching and Preachers* (Zondervan, 1971), p 182..

21 Timothy Keller, *Prayer: Experiencing Awe and Intimacy with God* (Penguin, 2014), p 229.

22 John Piper, "The Pleasure of God in the Prayers of the Upright" (sermon from Mar. 22, 1987), https://www.desiringgod.org/messages/the-pleasure-of-god-in-the-prayers-of-the-upright (accessed Nov. 30, 2023).

23 Portions of this chapter are further expanded in *The Pastor's Soul,* written by Brian Croft and Jim Savastio

(Evangelical Press, 2018) and *Pastoral Perseverance* by
Brian Croft and James Carroll (Evangelical Press, 2024).

24 For further reading, see *Pastoral Friendship: The Forgotten
Piece of a Persevering Ministry* by Michael A.G. Haykin,
Brian Croft, and James Carroll (Christian Focus, 2022).

25 To see the full explanation of my two-month sabbatical
and how it was presented to our congregation, see
Appendix A of *The Pastor's Soul* book.

26 Martyn Lloyd-Jones in *Spiritual Depression*.

27 These words were written by Michael Casey and
were found on a wall at Abbey of Gethsemani near
Bardstown, KY. Abbey of Gethsemani is one of the few
functioning silent monasteries that exists in the United
States.

28 Quote taken from http://www.unimedliving.com/men/
relationship/real-men-don-t-cry.html

29 Iain H. Murray, *Archibald G. Brown: Spurgeon's Successor*
(Edinburgh: Banner of Truth, 2011), p 98.

30 As above, p 144.

31 As above, p 145.

32 Portions of this chapter were taken from and/or greatly
expanded in *The Pastor's Soul* (Evangelical Press, 2018)
and *Pastoral Friendship* (Christian Focus, 2022).

33 https://www.merriam-webster.com/dictionary/intimate

34 Practical Shepherding is my ministry to other pastors,
which I continue to lead as my primary ministry focus.
For more information, go to www.practicalshepherding.
com.

35 Eugene Peterson, *On Living Well: Brief Reflections on
Wisdom for Walking in the Way of Jesus* (Waterbrook,
2021), p 42.

the good book

COMPANY

BIBLICAL | RELEVANT | ACCESSIBLE

At The Good Book Company, we are dedicated to helping Christians and local churches grow. We believe that God's growth process always starts with hearing clearly what he has said to us through his timeless word—the Bible.

Ever since we opened our doors in 1991, we have been striving to produce Bible-based resources that bring glory to God. We have grown to become an international provider of user-friendly resources to the Christian community, with believers of all backgrounds and denominations using our books, Bible studies, devotionals, evangelistic resources, and DVD-based courses.

We want to equip ordinary Christians to live for Christ day by day, and churches to grow in their knowledge of God, their love for one another, and the effectiveness of their outreach.

Call us for a discussion of your needs or visit one of our local websites for more information on the resources and services we provide.

Your friends at The Good Book Company

thegoodbook.com | thegoodbook.co.uk
thegoodbook.com.au | thegoodbook.co.nz
thegoodbook.co.in